Feedback has become a bit
culture. Most people hate ¦
everyone believes it is esse
develop. At last, a book that actually addresses this
honestly and openly, dismantling the myths, helping
us understand the psychology of feedback and, most
importantly, be better at having the conversations that
help us and others thrive at work.
**Karen Meager – organisational psychologist and author**

This book has helped me gain a deeper understanding of
my own reactions to giving and receiving feedback and
provided tools for navigating it more effectively.

It's a surprisingly easy read, using data and research
to help you understand not only how to give better
feedback, but also how to receive and process it in a
more constructive way. It goes beyond practical steps,
offering the 'why' behind it all, with real-life examples that
resonate.

I highly recommend this book to anyone looking to
improve their relationship with feedback, whether giving
or receiving. It's a valuable resource for understanding
your own reactions and harnessing the power of feedback
for growth.

I especially loved that it doesn't offer a one-size-
fits-all solution, exploring the various models we've all
encountered. Well-researched, thought-provoking and
applicable to everyone – even if some of it feels familiar,
it's all the more powerful for it.
**Sarah-Jane Allen – chief of staff, Google DeepMind**

This fabulous, compact book has practical tips for giving and receiving feedback, some of which I have implemented already. Difficult conversations are made easier when we are in the right frame of mind and able to hear what is and isn't being said. I found the tips inspiring and immediately useful. I liked the quotes that showed me how the advice has helped other people, demonstrating that it's not just theoretical. A great read that I shall be recommending to others.

**Dr Sam Powell – GP and GP trainer, appraiser and coach**

How is it that feedback can so often demotivate people rather than inspire them?

This is the question that Becky Westwood's excellent book answers. It's packed with practical exercises, tips and techniques to help people have better, more positive conversations about performance.

Even before we get to the main part, the contents list gives an indication of the straight-talking style of this practical, well-researched book.

The first sentence of the first chapter was a game-changer for me. From then on I was hooked. Even though I'm a manager with 30 years' experience, this book made me reconsider how I have been giving feedback and how I can approach it in the future to make sharing my perspectives with my staff an encouraging and inspiring experience.

**Peter Andrews – senior manager, local government**

# Can I Offer You Something?

Expert ways to overcome the
horrors of **organisational feedback**

Becky Westwood

**Can I Offer You Something?**
ISBN 978-1-915483-51-5 (paperback)
ISBN 978-1-915483-52-2 (ebook)

Published in 2024 by Right Book Press
Printed in the UK

A CIP record of this book is available from the British Library.

# Contents

# Foreword

It's great to finally see this book in print having discussed it and heard Becky's passion around the ideas in it for a number of years. It is also great to see this book in print *now*. It comes at a time when a fundamental shift is needed in how organisations engage in their people development, particularly in relation to feedback. I love the title as it sums up exactly the challenge I see with feedback, which often looks like, and is presented as, a friendly offer of helpful advice and guidance. However, all too often the feedback is nothing more than someone else's preferences or needs – a point that Becky expertly explores in detail with useful examples throughout her book.

Becky has long had a strong view, which I share, about the need to change the relationship with feedback in organisations. It's no surprise having worked with Becky for over ten years that she shares these views, her expertise and her experience in the same relaxed, accessible and humorous way that I have seen her do in her leadership coaching and training over many years. This style really helps you, as the reader, to connect with the ideas and concepts easily. The book invites you to think about feedback in a fundamentally different way, why change is needed and what you could consider doing instead.

My own interest in feedback and my frustration with it started over 30 years ago when I had my first encounter with it. At the time, it felt like it was important and I could see the potential benefit of getting the views of more experienced colleagues and managers. Sadly, I found myself generally left feeling confused, often that I was failing in some way and unsure what I should do with many of the comments I received. Where I could see that changes would be helpful, I was unsure how to implement them in a way that reflected me and aligned with my values. Since those early days, I have seen the increasing drive for a homogenised, overly processed approach to feedback as the biggest challenge with the feedback culture within organisations. This not only applies to feedback; it is happening in leadership and management development and training, and the negative impact on manager and leadership skills, confidence and ability has only got worse the last 30 years. Such was my own frustration with the organisational approach to training and development in my own corporate/organisational career that I have spent the last 20 years working with forward-thinking leaders and organisations to put the human being back into the process, make the advice practical and relevant to the person themselves and keep it real. This has been grounded in the three organisational and leadership books I have co-authored with Karen Meager, Real Leaders, Time Mastery and Rest. Practise. Perform. that all seek to make organisations and organisational development practical, grounded in reality and actionable. In that journey I had the great fortune to meet and then, for the last ten years, work with Becky to bring this to the world.

Becky and I have shared many a long discussion about the limitations and at times positively unhelpful ways in which feedback is used in organisations. We shared a view that all too often the apparent advice being given was really personal preference or things that should have been given as a direct management instruction dressed up as feedback. This book, and the research and expert advice that Becky shares in it, come at a very opportune time as I share her view that we need to get more real with feedback, see it for what it really is and look for better ways to support people to grow and develop.

The content of the book is the product of the new research Becky has undertaken in the last few years on feedback as part of her master's thesis. This research is enriched and brought to life by her expertise and experience in people development for over 20 years in a wide range of organisations. The basis of this book, Becky's research and expertise, has been used efficiently and effectively where it is necessary and relevant to help you, as the reader, question and update your understanding of how to use feedback – perspectives, as Becky more accurately calls them. There is a very natural flow between the theory and practical examples. This helps you to both understand what feedback is really about and suggest how to make tangible changes in your relationship with it that are helpful to you and those around you. What struck me as I read is that in addition to helping you change your relationship with feedback, it gives you an important understanding of how feedback is received and felt by others. The book is practical with ideas you can action immediately and others that have a longer-term implementation and impact exploration. The key point that I love, and Becky brings to life throughout the book, is the need to bring the human being back as the focus of feedback.

This book invites you to consider a new and updated approach to your own development and those around you and I hope you enjoy reading it as much as I did.

**John Mclachlan**, organisational psychologist and CEO, Monkey Puzzle Training

# Preface

'I love feedback' isn't a sentence you hear very often, and even as I wrote this book the irony wasn't lost on me that at times I was feeling anxious about getting feedback on a book about feedback and anxiety – we psychologists are humans too! Despite this, many people understand the benefits of hearing different perspectives. Everyone experiences feedback differently and, based on my own academic research into the relationship between feedback and anxiety, this book explores what can be learned from individuals with social anxiety and how their experiences can help anyone have a healthier and more purposeful relationship with feedback in an organisational setting.

# Part 1

## Feedback is hard (but it doesn't have to be)

# 1

# Introduction

What if you called feedback 'perspectives'? What if you said hello to the human in front of you and just had a conversation? What if you used perspectives to create possibilities?

As an organisational psychologist, trainer and coach, I've spent much of my career working with individuals, teams and leaders in organisations of varying sizes across the UK, Europe and the US. I've had many of my own opportunities to give and receive feedback and heard countless stories about the nerves, anxiety and fear people felt as they encountered feedback in their organisations.

The feelings described to me were inspired by experiences of both giving and receiving feedback, so I became curious about what made feedback so difficult for people. It's as if they become resigned to the fact that exchanging feedback is like an emotional rollercoaster that they must keep on riding. Underneath it all, people want to be recognised for their contributions, learn about opportunities to develop themselves or support the development of others. Through my research, I wanted to explore the possibility that exchanging feedback could be something different, something simpler, more purposeful and without the extreme emotional ups and downs of unnecessary anxiety.

The truth is that everyone feels anxious at different moments in their life – it's normal. In that sense, anxiety is universal – you don't need to have an anxiety problem to feel anxious. Everyone has their own personal relationship with feedback. Our upbringings, educational experiences, relationships and history all impact our attitude to feedback, how we process it and what we do with it. We'll explore all of this in detail later in the book.

In organisations, the two go hand in hand, as feedback often provokes anxiety in both the person providing it and the person receiving it. People providing feedback become preoccupied with not saying the wrong thing, not upsetting or offending the receiver and not demotivating them with their feedback. People receiving feedback become anxious about the unknown of what might be said, how to action any feedback and the vagueness of the feedback's content.

One of the main reasons that people find feedback challenging is that, for most, their work is more than work – it's part of who they are. It's not just something they show up and do for a few hours. For example, when someone says 'Your presentation could be better', people hear 'You could be better.'

Imagine you've always been worried about X during a presentation and then Y happens. You know you've messed up and are feeling rubbish about it – then your manager wants a debrief...

Imagine you're a manager who wants to support your team and you notice that someone's doing something in presentations that could stop them from doing so much better, but you're not sure why they do it or if they're even aware...

Exchanging feedback can end up feeling incredibly personal. The highs are engaging, motivating and encouraging. The lows can feel judgemental, confronting and disheartening. No wonder people feel anxious about doing it, and the anxiety makes the whole thing worse as people try to rush through it, avoid it or make up unhelpful stories about what they're experiencing. It becomes a vicious circle of pain and dread.

While organisations strive to address this by creating positive feedback cultures, they're mostly successful in principle rather than in practice. This leads to a lost investment of time and money for those organisations. They put resources and effort into designing feedback processes, investing in feedback tooling and provide training in how to give feedback – none of which will necessarily address the anxiety of sharing feedback or increase people's use of it. As a result, this translates into a lost opportunity for the development and recognition of their people.

If people continue to limit their interactions with feedback and don't give themselves an opportunity to practise the skills involved, on an individual level, people start to disengage with feedback. They avoid seeking it and giving it until it becomes a stressful and inescapable activity to undertake at the annual performance review. If, like many people in organisations, you go into feedback meetings with 'I just want to get it over with' ringing in your ears, you're likely to miss an opportunity to develop and this might create unintended people dramas that need to be solved later.

What if there were a different way?

The more I specialised in working with people with social anxiety, the more curious I became about how their experiences in the workplace compared to those without social anxiety.

If everyone experiences anxiety in some way when it comes to feedback, my goal was to provide people with an opportunity to learn from those whose anxiety experiences were more acute. I wanted to bring levity to a serious topic and make discussing it in the workplace more accessible. I'm not saying that everyone needs to disclose their anxiety at work, but it's possible to work with your anxiety to find out what it is you need and then use that awareness to help you have a conversation, ask a question and build a relationship with feedback that serves you.

This book is for managers, leaders, colleagues, providers and recipients of feedback in business and organisations. Whichever side of the feedback exchange you're on, sharing effective feedback is a collection of skills that, when done well, takes account of anxiety for all involved. These skills can be learned and I'll show you how.

If you want to support people with their growth or maximise your own development, this book can help you find practical strategies that work for you. Everyone experiences feedback differently and, based on my own academic research into the relationship between feedback and anxiety, the findings of which are explored in Chapter 3, this book explores what can be learned from individuals with social anxiety and how their experiences can help anyone have a healthier and more purposeful relationship with feedback in organisations.

# How to use this book

At any moment in your career, you could find yourself on either side of feedback. This book is about learning from academic research and individuals' lived experiences to improve how feedback is perceived and used by everyone for the benefit of those who want to use it for their development. If you're offering feedback, it's about increasing your confidence around the whole exchange, increasing effectiveness and feeling less anxious. If you're receiving feedback, it's about coming out of the feedback exchange feeling encouraged, valued and empowered.

As you progress through the book, I'll present you with findings from two recent studies that I conducted into the use of feedback in organisations. I'll explore three of the most common feedback models used in organisations and some feedback mnemonics – their strengths and limitations along with the myths surrounding feedback. In the chapters that follow, I'll unpack these myths in greater detail, offering insights into how they might show up for you and others so you can build up a holistic picture of the feedback dynamic.

Whether you're the provider or receiver, in Part 3 of the book there are some initial reflective questions for you to consider, to build up your awareness of your relationship with feedback. You'll also find exercises and techniques you can practise and actions you can take, based on your role in sharing feedback. These tools will help you to design your own personal approach to feedback and learn about what works for others to enhance its effectiveness for you and those you're working with.

I want you to have more choice about how you use feedback. Whatever past experience may have led you to believe, whatever you might have made it mean in your own mind or whatever you might have been told about feedback until now, if it's not useful and it's not serving you, put it to one side. Instead, give yourself permission to do something differently with feedback.

As you work through the chapters, you'll read about the experiences of some of my clients and research participants in their own words. All the quotes, examples and case studies have been used with permission and, to respect their confidentiality, the people involved can't be identified. In some of the examples, you might recognise moments where you've done or seen similar things; that's OK, we've all been there. The key is, if you can understand why they might have happened, you have a greater influence on changing how they happened and stopping some of them repeating in the future.

This book isn't solely intended for people who experience anxiety at work; instead it's for anyone who wants to learn from these individuals' experiences. It invites you to reconsider and reimagine your relationship with feedback, take feedback off its over-complicated pedestal and make it more accessible. It won't offer you another generic model of feedback but instead will support you in designing and putting into practice personal strategies to get the most out of your own and other people's perspectives in support of your goals.

# 2

# What did feedback ever do to you?

With one seemingly simple word, you can inspire so many different thoughts and reactions in people, and that word is: feedback.

As you read that word, are you reminded of that annual review when... [insert experience here], catapulted back to parents' evening when that teacher said..., reflecting on how you or the other person reacted when x was mentioned... or, depending on your musical preferences, you might just be recalling the love–hate noise that happens when musicians get creative with their instruments. Perhaps you're not thinking much at all and instead feeling excitement, curiosity, worry or even dread. You might be noticing an increase in your heart rate, sweaty palms or be bracing for impact. To all and any of these reactions, I first say: breathe.

Whatever your reaction to that word, it's just that – yours. It's personal and can often feel as if you're the only one who feels that way. However, at times, you're better at interacting with feedback than you might think. When you feel cold, you don't think twice about reaching for an extra layer; when you feel hungry, you look for something to eat; if you look outside and see that it's raining, you might grab a coat or umbrella before heading out. Your responses to these situations are considered sensible and you can be open about them. Yet there's something about feedback at work where it starts to get difficult – and if that's you, you're not alone.

The combination of reactions you experience will be unique to you in their intensity, effect and duration but the chances are you have more in common with others than you think, especially when it comes to feedback at work. It's well reported that feelings of anxiety at work are on the rise, with an 8 per cent increase in people experiencing anxiety symptoms at work in the past year (Champion Health 2024) due to the increasing and changing demands of the modern workplace (HR News 2022; Joseph 2021). When you feel low-level anxiety, it can be easier to brush it off as a moment of being silly, but these little pangs of anxiety can be distracting, affect your performance and get in the way of you doing what you want to do.

There are a whole range of relationships and roles that someone can take up at work. You might be reading this book as a leader, mentor, collaborator, colleague or manager, to name a few. All these roles offer the opportunity to both provide and receive feedback. These opportunities might present themselves during formal processes that happen within your organisation – for example, when someone is seeking a promotion or it's time to do annual reviews – or happen more organically throughout the year. In your organisation, you may be the provider of feedback, the receiver of feedback or both; either way people can put a lot of pressure on themselves or others to engage with it.

It's almost as if, over time, feedback has become the panacea to correcting, enhancing and maximising performance, and held up on a pedestal. In reality, it's a monolith for some that has become overcomplicated and inaccessible, and this can lead to feelings of frustration and overwhelm for all involved. As a result, for many, their relationship with exchanging feedback has become a muddied experience, a process that people feel trapped in and that they just try to get through or avoid.

Feedback can be hard, but it doesn't have to be.

The more you can understand why exchanging feedback is hard for you and others, the greater the choice you'll have to make some practical changes that make the whole experience more valuable for everyone. When feedback is done well, people can liberate themselves and others from the space between a rock and a hard place that causes unnecessary anxiety and step into any number of possibilities. Instead of feeling controlled by a single word, people can choose how they want to use feedback to help them realise their potential and achieve their goals.

# Why is feedback so challenging for people?

To answer this question fully, we need to look at three contributing influences: the origins of feedback, its use in organisations and people's individual experiences.

## The origins of feedback

Winding the clock back, the word feedback comes from the combination of two words: feed and back. Feed comes from the Old English fedan, which means 'to nourish'; and back from the Old English bæc, meaning 'backwards or behind'. The two words then met in the world of electrical science during the early 20th century and became feedback.

Its original use was to describe the transfer of data in closed electrical systems. A signal is sent out and the data that comes back is feedback. Then it evolved and began being used in connection with the regulation of processes or safety systems. The best example of this that we all likely know is the petrol pump. We put fuel in a car and when the tank is full, a feedback signal is sent so the pump shuts off to stop spillages and overfilling – keeping the system safe.

There's no universally agreed definition of the word feedback; in fact, it's a word that only became used in relation to people through theories of behavioural science and psychology around the 1940s and 1950s. Here the word feedback became focused on people and began being used in relation to the transmitting of information between humans. Since then, the definition has evolved to include a range of variations, and what has emerged is more than 35 words to describe different types of feedback that people can exchange: negative feedback, constructive criticism, reinforcement feedback, positive feedback, recognition feedback, feedforward and so on.

One of the downsides of all these different terms is that it can become confusing for both provider and receiver about what they're exchanging. Is it really feedback or is it something dressed up as feedback? It's also unclear who these labels serve – in my experience, it's highly unlikely that someone will walk up to another person and say 'I'm about to give you some constructive criticism...' If you go into a situation thinking you're about to give or receive constructive criticism, it will have an impact on how you behave.

Categorising feedback into different types doesn't serve the provider or recipient; it just makes the whole thing more complicated than it needs to be. The solution to this is to get clear on what feedback is and isn't, and that's why I advocate calling feedback what it really is – a perspective.

A perspective is about how you individually experience something, how you see, hear or feel what's going on both around you and within you. A perspective is not right or wrong, true or false, positive or negative; it just is. Wisdom comes from multiple perspectives and sharing your perspective and gathering that of others can be valuable for two main reasons.

1.  No two humans see the world the same way; your perspective is unique to you and so will always highlight novel ways of seeing, thinking about or approaching a situation.

2. We're not always brilliant at recognising our own strengths, limitations and opportunities for development, so a fresh pair of eyes can highlight new possibilities and choices.

If you think about the petrol pump example and what usually happens to people when they hear the word feedback, it's hard not to see the irony of the system shutting down to remain safe. In a way, the word fulfils its original 1940s definition, but when it comes to people, this shutting down can have unintended consequences for their wellbeing, development and performance.

## Feedback in organisations

Organisations invest time, energy and money in creating feedback processes, training employees and getting the latest feedback software and tooling. The global market for 360° feedback software alone was valued at just over $1 million in 2023 and is projected to grow to $2,136 million by 2030 (Fortune Business Insights 2024). Many organisations make these investments because they believe in their people and want to support them by creating a positive feedback culture – an environment in which all employees feel safe to share and receive feedback with each other openly and honestly, in the spirit of development.

While some organisations are successful in doing this, for many others it's in principle rather than in practice, and this is often the result of focusing on processes first. Processes are great for being able to provide standards, structure and reporting, but when it comes to feedback, they can become so overengineered that they prevent the thing they were put in place to achieve, which is simply to help people talk to each other.

Organisations often focus their L&D efforts on the people providing feedback. This typically means managers and leaders getting trained first. The problem with this is that it unfairly puts the responsibility of feedback in one place and upholds one of the organisational feedback myths I'll look at in Chapter 5. Sharing feedback is rarely a solo pursuit and ensuring one group of people are clear and trained on a process doesn't necessarily ensure feedback culture will follow.

In my work with different organisations and individuals, including the people who participated in my research, it wasn't lack of process or guidelines that got in the way of people sharing feedback. More often than not, it was their past experiences of a generic process or structure being inelegantly or unhelpfully 'done to them' that caused problems.

The more mechanised the tools, processes and guidelines that are put in place, the higher the feedback pedestal becomes. As a result, in many organisations, feedback becomes a hot topic only one or two times a year, namely annual review time (or however this is described in your organisation). It's the time of year when feedback becomes a 'have to' and this creates psychological pressure for both providers and receivers. In their research, Kluger and DeNisi (1996) highlighted that feedback delivered poorly and 'just because' can lead to decreases in performance.

## Research quotes

'In my previous position, feedback was collated and handed over once a year as part of an annual review, which made appraisal time very stressful for everyone – the person delivering and the person receiving. It felt like the only opportunity to share, so both parties would "fight" to get their view across and agreed. It didn't feel productive or particularly inspiring.'

'We're not yet comfortable being in a feedback culture and so the action has to be pushed, which then affects the inputs. I find it un-useful when it's the time of year where everyone puts in feedback but it's overly "nice" just so they get good comments back. It makes the entire process pointless as minimal growth can come from it.'

In lots of organisations, this review period seems to catch people off guard, even though it usually happens at the same time every year. Managers and leaders providing feedback become preoccupied with how they'll recall and recount a year's worth of work, capture it in meaningful sentences or paragraphs and then share it with others. People on the receiving end can be surprised by the feedback they're receiving and get frustrated as they hear about things that may have happened months before that, which they can no longer do anything about.

In my opinion, no one should be surprised by the content of their annual review, regardless of whether what they're receiving is considered positive or not. This doesn't rely solely on managers or leaders but on everyone to find ways to engage in feedback throughout the year – including giving feedback to yourself. I've had the privilege of sitting across from many talented people who say to me 'I haven't done that much this year – I should have done more.' When I ask them to elaborate on what they mean and what 'not doing that much' involved, I've heard people say they have organised first-of-their-kind conferences, contributed to new legislation, supported a colleague with their mental health, improved processes, developed strategies, started mentoring someone and more. But all of this highlights one of the biggest challenges for everyone involved when it comes to feedback: that by avoiding or limiting our interactions with it, we don't give ourselves the opportunity to reflect, practise and move beyond some of our own blockers. Most of this is linked to working on our personal relationship with feedback, and Chapter 6 onwards will show you ways to do this. Organisations can also play a role in improving this relationship. In Chapter 5, I'll bust some of the organisational myths that affect how people interact with feedback and look at ways to put individuals, not process, back at the centre.

In the spirit of Old English, if part of 'feed-back' is about nourishment, there's no better approach than encouraging the people in your organisation to talk directly to each other and understand what they and others need on an individual level when it comes to feedback.

## The individual experience

Feedback isn't a natural process for humans to engage in. You can attempt to be logical and say to yourself 'It's just a bit of feedback; don't worry about it', but the reality is quite different because you're emotional first, logical second. Giving and receiving feedback, particularly what might traditionally be referred to as negative feedback, can leave you feeling exposed or challenged.

When it comes to feedback, that feeling of 'I just want to get it over with' is normal because humans are hardwired to avoid feelings of discomfort. So, you work yourself up, the meeting room door flies open, the feedback is chucked in, one person does more of the talking than the other and everyone exits as quickly as possible. Phew, it's over! If you're on the receiving end of that experience, you might be left thinking 'What just happened?', and if you're the person giving the feedback, you might be left thinking 'I hope I was clear'. Either way, it's likely to have been an experience not to be repeated.

Ask anyone how they feel about feedback and they'll have an answer for you. In the course of my work, I've asked many people this question and it's been met with everything from an eye roll to a facepalm to an audible groan. The words that usually follow are 'it depends'. It depends if I've asked for it or not, how it's delivered, if I'm the person giving or receiving it, and the list goes on.

## Research quotes

Some 'it depends' quotes from my research include:
    'It depends how it's said and who it comes from...'
'If I know it's coming, it's much better, but it depends on that and who's giving it to me...'
'It depends, really, if I've asked for it or if it's just because you've been told to give it to me...'
'It depends. Done well, it's a gift, but in my experience, it usually goes badly...'
'It depends on my mood...'

It can also depend on the type of feedback being given. When it comes to feedback, people sit broadly in one of three groups:

1.   Those who say 'I love positive feedback; I don't like critical or constructive feedback.'

2.   Those who say 'Constructive feedback is useful; positive feedback is uncomfortable.'

3.   Those who don't particularly enjoy either.

Your overall relationship with feedback, the type you pay attention to and how you use it, is influenced by your past experiences. It stands to reason that if you've had repeated positive experiences with it, you might be more likely to use feedback in some way. If you've had unhelpful experiences or fewer experiences overall, you might be less inclined to do so.

## Research quote

'During a discussion between senior leaders in an organisation, the topic of motivation and feedback came up. To my surprise, and I think that of many in the room, one leader said, "I don't give my team feedback." When one person asked them to elaborate, they said, "Well, no one's ever given me feedback and I turned out fine. They're all smart people; they'll know if they are doing something well or not – they don't need me to tell them."'

When it comes to being the provider of feedback, some of the common problems or blockers people describe are:

→ concern about how the other person will react

→ fear of saying the 'wrong' thing

→ fear of no longer being liked by the recipient

→ believing you'll demotivate the person receiving feedback

→ unease about providing second-hand feedback

→ in extreme cases, concern that the person on the receiving end will leave a project, team or organisation if you call out their behaviour.

When it comes to being the receiver of feedback, some of the common problems or blockers people describe are:

→ concern about getting feedback that's too vague or ambiguous

- frustration about receiving feedback that's too late
- fear of being judged as 'too emotional' or 'too defensive' if you question the feedback
- fear of not being liked by the provider
- not having space to discuss the feedback
- in extreme cases, worry that the feedback will limit future opportunities due to the perception of them it may create in others.

All the blockers and problems listed above are likely to be rooted in fear, and when people feel fear, their threat detection system is triggered and they have three routes: fight, flight or freeze. I've spoken to many people in my work and research who have described the ways in which they have navigated their fight, flight or freeze response when receiving feedback, with varying degrees of success and grace. The common thing in all these experiences was that people were trying to achieve a sense of control: control of themselves, control of the other person or control of the process. While some people felt they'd achieved this, many recognised that due to their methods, it came at the expense of their wellbeing, their relationships and future opportunities to receive feedback.

People working in organisations want to contribute, be challenged by their work, learn, be valued and recognised for what they're doing. All of this involves becoming aware of how you're doing, aware of your desired outcomes and aware of where you are in your pursuit of them. Ultimately this all involves perspectives.

So, instead of feedback being this arduous thing that happens to you or that you have to do; something that costs you emotional and mental energy, time and effort; something that you might just ignore or might get ignored anyway – what if you reconsider your relationship with it? I'm inviting you to take the time to reflect on what feedback means to you personally and the current impact it has on you. By understanding your relationship with feedback, you can develop your self-awareness and design strategies to enable you to interact with it in a practical way to support development and enhance performance.

# 3

# The research

## What is anxiety?

Feelings of anxiety are more common than you might think, and they're not all bad. Anxiety is a natural human response that we all experience when we feel under threat – real or imagined. In a sense, experiencing low-level anxiety is a signal that our body is working correctly. Our flight, fight and freeze response is triggered and a sudden flood of chemicals into our system can help us feel more alert and enable us to act faster.

At one time in our evolution, this threat detection system had to be highly tuned for survival, but our systems haven't moved on much, so what happens now is: new type of threat, same old response. It's appropriate if a sabretooth tiger is coming at us, but perhaps less helpful when it's a feedback email. It's an automatic process that we have no control over.

Anxiety in the workplace is becoming increasingly common as people navigate their work–life rhythm, the demands of deadlines and changing priorities. In the second of my two research studies, 68 per cent of people said that they experienced anxiety at work.

Anxiety becomes a problem if it gets in the way of someone's ability to do the things they want to do. Unhelpful levels of anxiety can affect our decision making, general wellbeing, ability to process information and performance. For some, their experiences with anxiety may lead them to seek a specific diagnosis and support. The most common type of anxiety is social anxiety, which is often characterised by a persistent fear of social or performance-based activities where people may be evaluated. It's estimated that one in ten adults will experience the continued effects of social anxiety, with many receiving a formal diagnosis of social anxiety or social phobia (Andlin-Sobocki et al 2005; Marcin & Nemeroff 2003; Vincent 2023; World Health Organization 2023).

The average age of the onset of social anxiety symptoms is 13 years old. However, in these teenage years, the symptoms often get overlooked. The average delay in seeking treatment or support is 15–20 years from the first symptom, and this could in part explain why so many people receive a diagnosis as adults (NICE 2013). Two influences that can help us understand the delay in seeking support are that some people consider their social anxiety to be part of their personality or have concerns about the stigma of mental health affecting other people's perception of them (Amy 2016; Wittchen et al 1999).

The stigma of mental health in the workplace was one of the reflections from all the participants interviewed as part of my first research study, which is described in more detail later in this chapter. People didn't want to disclose anxiety for fear that they'd be judged, have work taken away from them or not be considered for high stakes opportunities – essentially that people may do their thinking for them.

When you think about someone who experiences social anxiety, you wouldn't be alone in thinking about potential challenges such as public speaking, being at networking events or in crowded rooms. For some, this is accurate, but the reality is that people also describe challenges with having lunch with colleagues or putting forward their ideas in team meetings and during one-to-ones. I've spent much of my career working with people who experience social anxiety, and one of the common things that came up for them was how difficult they found feedback at work – but this didn't stop them from wanting it.

The experiences people describe include a range of physical, emotional and cognitive symptoms such as rapid heart rate, more internal self-talk and shaking legs. While some of these symptoms may be similar to those experienced by someone without social anxiety, the key difference is that for someone with the condition, the experience is often acute and more intense. One of my clients told me that his experience is 'like having the same dial of worry as everyone else but it's cranked up to 11'.

Whether you're the provider or receiver of feedback, with identified anxiety or not, the fact that feedback at work provokes feelings of anxiety for most people is one of life's worst-kept secrets. Organisations do well-intended work to address this by providing training and resources for people but often this training is focused on the people providing the feedback. If people continue to think about only one side of this dynamic, it will keep the anxiety seesaw in motion – and no one wants to be on that for long.

By taking findings from research that looks at the real-life experiences of people with and without anxiety, you can build your understanding of this anxiety and make the whole process of exchanging feedback more straightforward and purposeful.

# My research findings

The expanse of research into the use of feedback in organisations and the relationship between feedback and social anxiety is vast. Studies have typically been experimental and quantitative, focused on one element of the experience: the effects of different types of feedback, the source of the feedback, its structure, how it's delivered and beyond. One of the common challenges when looking at the effectiveness of feedback on performance in organisations is that it's difficult to isolate these things from each other in practice.

I wanted to build on this established set of theories and explore something very practical outside a controlled experiment environment. With that in mind, the goal of my first piece of research was to understand the real-life experiences of people with social anxiety when it comes to feedback in the workplace. It was grounded in the reality of the organisations they worked in and looked at their total experience, including the feedback conversation itself and anything related that happened for them before and after it took place.

I was particularly interested in researching the experiences of people aged between 28 and 36, as this could be a realistic time frame when symptoms and experiences with social anxiety peak. It's the resulting age range when you add the mean onset age and average delay in seeking support for social anxiety.

People who took part in the study all self-identified as experiencing social anxiety and were interviewed using semi-structured interviews that included space to freely narrate their experiences. As the foundation, the interviews used a consistent set of questions which had been given ethical approval by the psychology ethics committee at Essex University. The interviews were audio recorded and transcribed, then analysed using a quantitative research approach called interpretative phenomenological analysis (Westwood 2023).

The purpose of my second study was to look at the experiences of people interacting with feedback where they didn't necessarily have a diagnosis of anxiety. I was curious to see how their experiences would compare to those in the first research. The second study consisted of an online questionnaire that included both multiple-choice and free-text responses. Some of the questions mirrored those from the first piece of research, along with the additional option for people to offer suggestions for improvements on how feedback is used in organisations. The multiple-choice questions were statistically analysed and the free-text responses were analysed using another qualitative method called thematic analysis.

# Research demographics

|  | **Study 1** | **Study 2** |
|---|---|---|
| Gender | 66.7% female<br>33.3% male | 62.5% female<br>35% male<br>2.5% non-binary |
| Age | 100% were aged<br>28–36 years | 22.5% were aged 25–34<br>30% were aged 35–44<br>30% were aged 45–54<br>12.5% were aged 55–64<br>5% were aged over 64 |

The people who participated in both studies came from a range of professional backgrounds including public sector, law, operations, research, project management and engineering. They were working in roles across Europe, the US, UK and Asia and at different levels of their organisations from experienced senior leaders to those earlier on in their careers. The demographic statistics of the participants across the two studies are shown in the table above.

The most surprising finding from the first research was that 100 per cent of people knew how feedback could be best delivered to them – what would be most helpful to minimise their anxiety. When asked if they'd shared these preferences with colleagues, a manager or a leader, 100 per cent of them said no. The main reason given for this was concern about how they could share these preferences without admitting that they experienced anxiety. Interestingly, in the second study, 87.5 per cent of respondents also had preferences for how they'd like to receive feedback. If receiving feedback is hard, it seems giving feedback on feedback is another thing entirely.

During both studies, people described a number of different challenges that they experienced, and for those in the first study these often started well before a word of feedback was even uttered and lasted well beyond any conversations they had. I heard stories of people whose anxiety started the moment they received the invitation to the feedback meeting and stayed with them long after the meeting had finished; stories of people experiencing physical symptoms such as migraines that kept them off work; and moments when people felt so preoccupied by the expectation of what was about to happen that it obstructed their ability to concentrate or make decisions in their roles. Many people didn't feel as if they could talk about their anxiety at work.

## Research quotes

'I do get anxious, nervous, but I try to ignore that and just give them what they want, and do it the way they want. Even if I don't agree with it, I don't tell them [about my anxiety]. That's something that would be very looked down upon. That's something that people would really judge you for, and maybe think you're not a competent employee.'

'No, I would not share that [anxiety] with them because it's, it's the stigma of mental health... they will not receive it very well. And I would not want them to think that there's something more serious wrong with me. It's very hard.'

The participants also had positive experiences with feedback and valued it when it was done well, in a timely way and with care and consideration. They talked about investing in their development, a desire to get better at what they were doing and being able to perform in a sustainable way. Many described wanting to provide a valuable contribution to whatever their teams or organisations were trying to achieve; the piece they felt was missing was that they didn't always know how they were doing.

## Research quotes

'When it's been done well for me, it provides the possibility to learn and to get some valuable input. Tough, I prefer giving it than receiving it.'

'Something that can be useful information and data to help you focus your time and effort on skills and develop and correct issues.'

'It's a chance to see how what I do is perceived by others and see if what I'm doing is having a good impact on the team's goals.'

'My team tend to respond positively if it's based on evidence and not opinions. There's an art of delivering feedback and it has to have a certain level of emotional intelligence.'

While these positive feedback experiences were few, people wanted more of them. Many had strategies that they used to support themselves during the exchange of feedback and recommendations for improving how feedback is used in organisations.

## Participants on the use of feedback in organisations

'Make giving feedback a natural exchange between employees.'

'Ask employees what they want or need and find useful, rather than doling out unsolicited feedback based on an agreed process.'

'Stop forcing it! Work out why it's important to the person receiving it and offer it to them.'

'Do more of it. In the moment. But only if you invest in and develop a culture of psychological safety first.'

'It should just be part of the culture rather than as part of very specific processes, eg performance management or post-project reviews, etc.'

'More spontaneous and less formal.'

'Encourage it more by leading by example.'

# Research themes

The overall themes that emerged from my studies were as follows.

→ **Relational not transactional.** The participants talked about their aspiration for feedback to be based around human connection first. They described the significance of interaction, having a chance to talk, time to reflect and experiencing something based on their preferences rather than a prescribed process. Ultimately they wanted it to just be two humans having a conversation.

→ **Managing the physiological effects of anxiety.** All participants in Study 1 explained how important it was to them to manage the effects of anxiety while receiving feedback. They wanted to exchange feedback and at the same time they didn't want to disclose their anxiety. Instead, they chose to use different techniques and practices to manage their state before, during and after. On occasion, participants felt overwhelmed and their techniques were less effective. In these moments they made different choices about how to either delay or avoid what they perceived to be difficult conversations to reduce psychological pressure.

→ **The challenge of language and ambiguity.** When talking about language, participants described the influence of the words used by others towards them as well as the language they used towards themselves. People found ambiguous or 'fluffy' language used by others particularly difficult as they couldn't always get the point of what was being said or asked. This often led them to fill in the gaps and reach unhelpful conclusions or assumptions – usually that they were in serious trouble or had upset someone else.

As you progress through the rest of the book, these themes will be explored in more detail, and I'll offer you some practical tools and strategies to use for yourself and with others.

# Part 2

## Models, mnemonics and myths

# 4

# Feedback models and mnemonics: the good, the bad and the ugly

We've likely all had those moments when we enter a conversation with the best intention in the world to be as clear as possible, but then something takes us off course, the conversation gets derailed and unintended words fall out of our mouth. The reality is we all have these elegant and less elegant moments – we're all human, after all. However, when it comes to feedback, this can leave both the provider and receiver feeling confused, anxious, frustrated and sometimes overwhelmed or underwhelmed by the exchange.

It's unsurprising, then, that there's a wide range of models and tools for structuring and providing feedback. In doing the background reading for my first piece of research, I came across more than 15 different feedback models, all with two main aims:

1. Offering a simple framework that people providing feedback can use to organise and put together their messages.
2. Ensuring these messages are delivered in a clear and structured way so the receiver builds awareness and understands what's expected of them.

To create a positive feedback culture for their people, many organisations zoom in on a model and invest time, money and energy in promoting its use. With more and more options available for organisations and feedback providers to choose from, it's worth taking a closer look at some of these models. Three of the most widely known models of feedback in organisations are the feedback sandwich, the SBI or SAID model and 360° feedback.

# Feedback sandwich

This well-known model, also referred to as the hamburger method, the compliment sandwich and the sandwich technique, was popularised in business in the 1980s. The principle of the model is simple and grounded in the idea that critical feedback or constructive criticism can be softened for the benefit of the recipient by putting it between two compliments – hence the use of sandwich in its many name variations. Although some name changes have attempted to move the model on from its roots – for example, the CRC model: commend, recommend, commend (Broderick 2023) – the principles stayed the same.

Despite its commonly used colloquial name, the 'shit

sandwich', this structure is not all bad. The one thing this model does well is that it encourages the person giving feedback to be specific about what they've observed and offer examples. This can be useful for the people receiving feedback to be able to contextualise what they're hearing and can eliminate the wishy-washy 'just be more...' or 'be less...' that receivers often find vague and unhelpful. The problem is that only part of the content is usually specific – the filling.

## Example of the feedback sandwich

'You did a really great job of getting the working group going, but you were a bit rude when you facilitated the meeting – you rushed people and your agenda still ran over. Do less of that next time. Overall, though – well done and keep going with the project.'

As in the example, the challenge with this model is that the main point of the sandwich is the filling, and everyone knows it. The bread becomes surplus to requirements, often being added just to make the whole thing less ugly and more palatable. In trying to find enough complimentary points to balance the criticism, the provider's initial and parting 'high five' or 'well done' can become highly generalised and come across as disingenuous. This can undermine any meaningful content and have an unhelpful effect on the relationship between provider and receiver.

The receiver can be quick to dismiss the compliments, instead bracing themselves for the message they suspect is coming. I like to call this 'boomerang suspense' – that moment when the compliment is thrown out but you hold your breath, waiting for the criticism to swing back around and clip you on the side of the head. While the criticism may never come, people still brace for its impact, believing that it will; during this bracing, any genuine messages of appreciation, praise or learning can get lost.

For good reason, this is not a model that many organisations consciously invest in or advocate for today because it's not a particularly nourishing sandwich. But its use was so propagated throughout businesses and organisations in previous years that many people are aware of it and so unconsciously fall into the trap of using it or expecting it.

# SBI and SAID models

The Situation, Behaviour, Impact (SBI) model from the Center for Creative Leadership and the Situation, Action, Impact, Do (SAID) models are two of the most popular feedback frameworks. In both, the feedback is structured around describing three main points: the situation, the behaviour or action, and the impact of that behaviour. The SAID model invites the provider to go one step further and offer the receiver a Do – a recommendation for something they should do more of or should start doing.

One of the benefits of these models is that they encourage the provider to concentrate on one type of feedback, offering positive or critical feedback, but not both at the same time. The intention is that feedback offered via the SBI or SAID frameworks is non-judgemental and can support the receiver in not only reflecting on their behaviour but also understanding its impact in a specific context. When used well, these models become particularly useful for 'in the moment' feedback that comes during or shortly after the live situation.

## Example of the SBI model

'Susan, in the team meeting we had this morning, you interrupted me twice and I felt like you were dismissing my opinion.'

The challenge with these two models is that, when not carried out well, the intention behind the behaviour can be assumed or inferred by the provider and the recipient can be left feeling responsible for the provider's feelings, neither of which are useful nor accurate. In the example above, which follows the SBI structure, meaning is being made of Susan's behaviour. Did Susan interrupt or did she speak at the same time? The difference is subtle but important. When behaviour is described subjectively, or intent is assumed in either direction, it's likely to be met with defensiveness and take the discussion in a less productive direction.

In an extension of SBI, an additional 'I' is added, taking it to Situation, Behaviour, Impact, Intent (SBII). This is a positive step to address the problems that can arise when assuming intent, but the challenge of accurately and objectively describing behaviour is the same.

# 360° feedback

Although 360° feedback is prominent in many modern organisations, its roots extend back to a concept called 'multi-rater feedback', which was used in the military more than 100 years ago. It was in the 1950s that the business world was introduced to the approach (Bracken et al 2016; Fleenor & Prince 1997).

Today, 360° feedback is used in numerous organisations, with some having a formal process and specific tool in place and others encouraging people to use the principles of the approach in a self-directed way. The process involves someone collecting feedback from a variety of people, which might include their team, people they collaborate with and people who structurally hold more senior and junior positions within the organisation.

When done well, for the receiver of feedback, the 360° approach can be a useful way to gain insights and build awareness of how others perceive them in different situations and calibrate that against their own perceptions. If they then have time and support to make sense of the feedback, it can inspire choice about what development steps they may want to take and offer some recognition for things they're doing well.

In many organisations, this type of feedback is completed anonymously and in writing, often giving people more time to consider and prepare what they want to say. For the provider of feedback, it can reduce their concern about the recipient's reaction, rather than if they were to deliver it in person, creating space to say the things that need to be said.

Of course, the most obvious challenge with this is that, when people know they can share their opinions freely and anonymously, sometimes it can give people carte blanche to spill a big bucket of judgement. If the receiver receives lots of contradictory opinions and viewpoints, the feedback will potentially stop being useful and instead become overwhelming and confusing.

### Research quote about 360° feedback

'360 is the WORST! I've seen lots of negative outcomes to individuals' mental health when this is handled badly. People will write troll-style comments in an anonymous 360, forgetting or not caring that the individual will read it.'

# Feedback mnemonics

There are a plethora of mnemonics available alongside feedback models that focus on the structure of feedback and are intended to offer simple prompts and reminders on how to approach giving and receiving feedback. Some examples include:

- The Five Rs of giving or receiving feedback: Request, Receive, Reflect, Respond, Resolve (Razzetti 2023)

- The three Cs of giving feedback: Clarity, Contextual meaning and Composure (Sherf 2023).

- ABCDEFG IS: Amount of information, Benefit of the trainees, Change behaviour, Descriptive language, Environment, Focused, Group check, Interpretation check and Sharing information (Bhattarai 2007).

- The four Rs of receiving feedback: Respond, Record, Reflect, React (Bock 2018)

While the intention may be simplicity, when you look into the details of the steps they're describing and the ambiguity of some of the prompt words, many of the mnemonics are anything but simple. Just like the variety of words used to classify the different types of feedback, another simple internet search will highlight the potentially confusing assortment of mnemonics available.

In some organisations they develop their own mnemonics or adopt one and look to embed it into their feedback culture. Perhaps one of the most widely known examples of this is the 4 As approach used at Netflix, which includes these steps: aim to assist, make it actionable, appreciate, and accept or discard. When used well, organisational mnemonics can create a 'common language' approach to sharing feedback, where everyone in the organisation is somewhat familiar with how feedback goes. However, in the course of my work I have heard stories where applying these mnemonics and the drive to always look for a feedback-sharing opportunity has had ugly consequences.

The main purpose of all these feedback models is to give a clear and consistent structure for providers to follow when shaping their feedback and to ensure the recipient has a clear understanding of what's expected of them. In a way, they all overpromise on these aims. As with all models and tools, when it comes to their effectiveness, the big proviso is 'if they're done well' or 'if they're used well'.

## Case study about mnemonics

When talking with Marcus he recalled a video interview where at the end the interviewer said that feedback was an important part of the organisation's culture. They saw every interaction as an opportunity for feedback with their AID approach: Action, Impact, Desired Behaviour. With that the interviewer began to tell Marcus that the lighting was bad and not professional and his shirt was 'not something I would have chosen for an interview'.

Marcus was not sure what to do in that moment but suffice to say when offered the role later that week he declined. It was not a culture or organisation that he wanted to join.

Consistency in providing feedback is difficult to achieve and in some sense a bit of a pointless endeavour as feedback isn't something you give or receive in a vacuum. Each different combination of provider and recipient brings together a unique set of individual preferences, and it's on these preferences that feedback conversations should be built.

If you've found a model or mnemonic that particularly works for you, that's great. The key is, does it also work for the other person? There is no one-size-fits-all approach.

# 5

# Feedback myths: the magnificent seven

When it comes to people doing what they do, the two biggest drivers affecting our behaviour are our values – the things that are important to us – and our beliefs – the things we believe to be true about ourselves, the people around us and the world at large. Our beliefs can be both empowering and limiting and, as someone once said to me, the great thing about beliefs is that we believe them, but the challenge with beliefs is that we believe them – ie they're not factually accurate.

As we interact with and take in the world around us through our senses, it isn't possible to pay attention to all the available information and data present – there's simply too much for our brains to cope with. So, we unconsciously process the information by deleting, distorting and generalising it through a number of filters, two of which are our values and beliefs. This allows us to disregard anything that isn't unconsciously important to us and consciously focus on the bits that are.

These filters are unique to everyone and the filtering process happens internally, so it's not immediately visible to others. But you'll have seen the outcome of this process if you've ever asked someone at the end of a film 'Did you like the bit when...?' and you're met with a blank face and the response 'I didn't see that bit'. Simply put, if it's not important to you, you won't take in the data.

No one else has the same values and beliefs as you. This is important when it comes to feedback as the filtering you do through your values and beliefs helps you to evaluate behaviour before and after it happens. This is in part why two people can observe the same behaviour and each person will describe or label it differently: confident vs arrogant, direct vs assertive, shy vs reflective.

When thinking about feedback, we all have our own personal beliefs that will influence how we interact with it, and I'll look more closely at these in Chapter 6. Alongside our individual beliefs, there are some common myths surrounding feedback that can often show up in organisations. Myths are generalisations that are constructed over time and subtly changed as they're passed from person to person. Like beliefs, they become truths, accepted by people as they see them play out in an organisation's culture and in people's behaviour. These feedback myths quickly become a factor in how feedback is used or not used within an organisation. By under-standing them you have an opportunity to consciously choose how to engage with them.

# 1. Feedback is a one-way street

The first myth is that feedback is a one-sided event, a monologue. The person providing the feedback shares their take on what to do differently or what needs to change, and the person receiving feedback just sits back and takes it on board. This can lead to the feeling that feedback is being done to that person or dumped on that person, and people receiving feedback in this way can start to pull away from the content, the person offering it or the organisation. People who provide feedback in this way may start to notice over time that they get asked to share their perspectives less often.

## Research quote

'I once asked one of my colleagues, "Can I offer you something?" I was so anxious about telling them my feedback and how they might react that before they had a chance to answer that question, I just started essentially word vomiting on them – pouring out all my thoughts and ideas on how they could improve and change. And then I left.

'The person told me later they felt bombarded, like I just dumped the feedback on them, and they weren't ready. They asked if I could give them the feedback again in writing. I thought I'd avoided the discomfort by getting it out there quickly, but then I just had to do it all over again – brilliant.'

When this myth plays out in behaviour, it often leads to feelings of disconnection.

Feedback is, in fact, a two-way street, with a roundabout, traffic lights, a zebra crossing and a parking spot. What I mean is that giving feedback is a conversation that goes back and forth at a pace that suits everyone. It's an opportunity to share points of view and listen openly. When feedback is offered with empathy, people will be more likely to stay present and engaged in the exchange. This is what most people are seeking when it comes to feedback – the human connection.

# 2. The universal formula

The second myth is about finding the one 'right' way to give feedback, which could be finding the right model, the right process or the right regularity. People in organisations can be encouraged to use a particular model, structure or rhythm that's chosen by the organisation. Alternatively, some people may lean on their own personal experience to choose how they engage with feedback. Either way, this can lead to the belief that there's a one-size-fits-all approach, and that can cause people to exchange feedback in a way that isn't authentic to them or well suited to the people they're engaging with and potentially result in having too much or too little feedback that's hard to process.

## Research quote

'Be authentic and genuine in the delivery of feedback. Understand how the person best learns and receives feedback.'

When this myth plays out in behaviour, it often leads to feelings of overwhelm or underwhelm.

As an example, for people providing feedback, if the 'universal formula' in their organisation is that feedback happens once a year, they might feel overwhelmed by the volume of feedback requests coming in at the same time. If they invest time, energy and a few moments of anxiety in preparing the content of the feedback and then the recipient chooses not to do anything with it, they might feel underwhelmed by the response to all their effort. Equally, for the recipient, if the 'universal formula' in their organisations is defined by a particular feedback model or the preferences of their manager, they may have feedback delivered in a way that isn't useful to them, again leading to potential overwhelm or underwhelm.

It's useful to consider that, if it were true that there's a one-size-fits-all approach, why do so many feedback models exist? The reality is that there's no universal way to give or receive feedback, but there's likely to be a right way for you. Everyone experiences feedback differently, and the more you can understand about your preferences and share those with people, the greater the benefits you'll get from exchanging perspectives.

# 3. Asking questions is a sign of defensiveness

The third myth is that, as the recipient, asking questions when someone is sharing feedback demonstrates defensiveness or can be perceived as making excuses and justifications. This can lead to situations where people don't have the specifics they need to fully process the information being shared with them. In combination, myths one and three can become self-perpetuating. If feedback is a one-way street and asking questions is not OK, then it's unlikely the feedback exchange will be an exchange at all.

Humans are meaning-making machines and, in the absence of meaning, we usually make it up – with varying degrees of accuracy. So, if the feedback discussion is vague or ambiguous, either person can then end up leaving without the clarity they need to take any next steps – or, perhaps worse, having assumed they know what the other person means, using their time and energy in a futile way to action the 'wrong' thing.

### Research quote

'I once had a very bad experience of feedback in a 360° appraisal where "start, stop, continue" was used and I got the same comments on things to start and stop, which was confusing and who could I ask about it? On reflection, it just shows how subjective feedback can be!'

When this myth plays out in behaviour, it often leads to feelings of uncertainty.

I once worked with a client who was given the feedback 'You need to be more collaborative'. Thinking they understood what the provider meant by collaborative, they spent a lot of time feeling unsure and, given their current workload, worried about how they could take on more projects, meet more people and attend more meetings. When I asked them how they knew that's what the provider meant by 'be more collaborative', they replied, 'I don't know that for sure, but I can't ask, they'll think I'm an idiot.'

Asking questions to clarify information can be done respectfully when in rapport with the other person, demonstrates curiosity and can help you build awareness of self and others. When it comes to feedback, the clearer you can be about the perspectives being shared will decrease the likelihood of unhelpful meaning-making.

# 4. Feedback is a call to action

The fourth myth is that feedback is always something to be actioned. It could involve 'continue doing', 'start doing' or 'stop doing' something. This is often where feedback unfairly gets much of its bad reputation. Directions or instructions are presented as feedback and, as a result, the consequences of taking action or not taking action are ambiguous. This usually happens because the person giving feedback wants to avoid a conversation where they might be perceived as micro-managing. Things can become unclear and receivers can busy themselves trying to action everything or action things that may not be a priority. This is particularly problematic if they've received lots of conflicting feedback.

**Research quote**

'I find that when receiving feedback, I'm more likely to take action if it's made as a suggestion for improvement rather than an instruction, which I can sometimes take as criticism and be defensive.'

When this myth plays out in behaviour, it often leads to feelings of frustration.

If a direction or a 'you have to act' is presented in an inferential or unclear way, recipients may infer there's a choice about doing or not doing where there isn't one. If they don't act on the request, this can lead to missed deadlines, missed opportunities, repeated meetings and repeated conversations. Ultimately, this can become equally frustrating for both the provider and recipient.

Feedback should be about creating choice – offering someone a perspective on something so they can choose what they do with it: learn, change, act, react, disregard, take it on board as a moment of recognition, and so on. The key is that whatever they choose to do or not do, they're not penalised.

# 5. 'Critical' feedback is the most useful

The fifth myth is that, when it comes to supporting people's development and performance, critical feedback is the most useful. This often goes hand in hand with the notion that people know they're doing a good job, so they don't need to be told. This type of approach can be demotivating and disheartening for people on the receiving end and adds to the perception that feedback is a threat.

Plenty of research (Belschak & Hartog 2009; Zenger 2018) has looked at how to position critical feedback to mitigate this, which led to the development of models such as the feedback sandwich method and the praise to criticism ratio (Losada & Heaphy 2004). This ratio, 6:1, suggests that you should offer someone six pieces of praise for every criticism; however, the research behind this ratio has been called into question by the original publishing journal and other business writers (Ferguson 2014; Friedman & Brown 2018; Brown 2021).

## Research quote

'Keep the conversation going – teams need to see this kind of verbal engagement to get comfortable with both getting recognition as well as seeing how they can grow (both as individuals and as a group). There's an immaturity with the topic (that comes with pride/ego) that identifying an area of development is an insult; we need to step away from this and recognise that we can all always improve and there's no shame in that. We can start by doing it together.'

When this myth plays out in behaviour, it often leads to feelings of guardedness or wariness.

As you saw with the feedback sandwich in the previous chapter, if people are expecting to receive criticism, they'll either avoid feedback or be on their guard waiting for it. This type of feedback is often felt deeply by people as it can come across as a judgement about who they are rather than a reflection of what they have or haven't done.

Positive and negative feedback can be equally uncomfortable, motivating, challenging and encouraging. It's important that feedback works for the person on the receiving end – after all, that's who it's for. The key is understanding for what purpose you want to offer or receive feedback and then use this to focus your efforts on either how you might offer the feedback or when and whom you might seek it from.

# 6. Feedback should come from the top

The sixth myth is that feedback should come from the top and that people take it more seriously if it comes from someone in a position of power, leaving feedback the responsibility of managers or leaders within an organisation. This not only pushes the burden of providing feedback in one direction, but it also limits the range of perspectives and possibilities someone will engage with.

For managers or leaders of large teams and individuals working in cross-functional projects, this approach to feedback can be particularly stressful as they may not be close to the day-to-day work. Giving feedback can become a process within a process as they often need to request feedback from others and then offer it second hand to their teams. If people only look to those above them for feedback, they may miss the opportunity to hear perspectives from people potentially closer to their work, other experts, peers or those who hold more junior positions in the organisation.

**Research quote**

'The people that work really closely with me and I've got a personal relationship with because we work so closely together, I think their feedback is far more important to me than say, even my manager, who I don't have that sort of relationship with. Professionally, I have respect for my manager, but we don't work closely on things. I think there's a more intrinsic relationship that you get from that personal connection and that makes the feedback from them more relevant and useful for me.'

When this myth plays out in behaviour, it often leads to feelings of pressure.

Gaining perspectives through different work relationships offers more diverse insights into behaviours, actions, reactions and performance that a manager or leader may not be present for. Importantly, always looking for feedback from one source might also lead someone to discount the option of taking the time to reflect on their own performance and provide feedback to themselves.

# 7. People don't really want or need feedback

The seventh myth is that people don't really want or need feedback. This myth is upheld by the misconception that people know when they're not at their best and when they are. When not at their best, they don't want someone else coming along and pointing it out, and when they are at their best, they know they're doing a good job so don't need to be told.

Likewise, if people don't act on feedback (and remember, they don't have to), the provider can start to think 'What's the point of giving it?' and they end up doing it less. The receiver then thinks 'They don't give or like giving me feedback, so what's the point of asking?' Back to the provider, who then says to themselves 'They don't ask for feedback; they probably don't want it.' And so they both go round in circles, conveniently avoiding each other and the topic of feedback.

## Research quotes

'If it's an area I'm passionate about, feedback can be anxiety inducing to deal with but if I'm not good at something or new to it and have a chance to develop, I'm more welcoming and open to it.'

'Feedback needs to be done regularly. If someone writes a good email (or has done some interesting research), a simple reply with "well done" really helps, even if you then might have some suggestions for improvements. Saving everything for the monthly one-to-one or even appraisal doesn't give the individual the chance to incrementally grow.'

When this myth plays out in behaviour, it often leads to feelings of neglect.

Based on the participants in my studies, people do

want feedback; they just don't want badly delivered, unclear or low-quality feedback. They want feedback that supports them in accomplishing their goals, helps them grow and provides meaningful recognition for their contributions in a timely way.

The more these myths are left to play out over time, the further embedded into an organisation's culture they become. These myths become truths and, as we see them potentially role modelled by providers and receivers of feedback around us, we're more likely to copy them rather than take a moment to question them.

Given that myths and beliefs aren't factually accurate, that they may be limiting beliefs and have a strong influence on your behaviour, the question to ask yourself now is: how do I really know what I think I know about feedback?

# Part 3

## Redesigning your relationship with feedback

# 6

# It's just two humans having a conversation

For many people, work has become so entangled with their life that they find it hard to separate themselves from what they do. In effect, their work has become part of who they are, closely tied to their identity and values; it's become something more than just a collection of skills that they show up and use.

While there's nothing wrong with this per se, when it comes to feedback it's no wonder the conversations can get tricky as feedback can be felt so deeply. You'll hear someone say 'That could've gone better', 'That way didn't work for me' or 'That was brilliant'; it's as though those feedback words go into our system and hit us straight in our identity.

Once you consider this, it makes sense why you often take the 'just rip the bandage off' or 'let's pretend it's not happening' strategy to get through sharing feedback as quickly as possible. But these approaches can lead to the whole thing feeling transactional and people can start to disconnect from the content of the feedback, others in the feedback exchange and, in some cases, the organisation. The exchange becomes something other than an exchange, which is the very thing that most people are seeking.

Across the two pieces of research I've conducted, 82 per cent of respondents wanted feedback to be relational. Most people want to move away from the experiences captured earlier in Myth 1 (feedback is a one-way street) and move the feedback conversation from monologue to dialogue – a conversation where people first understand the human in front of them.

## Research quote

### Provider of feedback

'You're trying to express something to another human, right? And what's the purpose there? Because you're trying to deliver something and you want them to listen, not just hear you, but listen. So, for me, I will think through the communication approach. I think that the labour of care to that other human is quite important. And also, I believe, that labour of care is the key so that they can really receive your message. They understand who you are, and you understand who they are and how they're going to take in the feedback.'

**Recipient of feedback**

'To just see the expression on the person's face and, you know, read the emotional intelligence. I feel like it's much better if it could be happening with a face-to-face. Yeah, I think it would be much better, especially working in a diverse organisation. With different cultures there's much to see because everybody has different backgrounds, and it's much better to interact with the person in front of you to just, you know, see them and know them, know when to stop and when to continue.'

In the following chapters, I'll share a number of practical strategies you can use in the moment when exchanging feedback. First, let's look at the big picture.

Changing your relationship with feedback requires you to understand where you're starting from. Humans are creatures of habit and if the things you've done before are getting 'OK' results, you're likely to keep on doing them. When you understand why you do something, you'll have a greater chance of changing how you do it. For this to happen, you need to start with understanding and owning your relationship with feedback: your personal beliefs, what you focus on and what the human in front of you needs when it comes to sharing perspectives.

# Your personal beliefs

These are generalisations you make about the world and trust to be true. They have a significant role to play when it comes to your behaviour, the things you perceive you can and can't do and, unless you've done some personal development work, you may not have had the opportunity to explore or evaluate them. Some of the beliefs you could hear or even say that get in the way when it comes to feedback include the following.

When I'm providing feedback:

- ➡ I'm not good at giving feedback.
- ➡ My team/that person knows how they're doing.
- ➡ People don't need it because I don't need it.
- ➡ I can't say x because I'll offend or upset someone.

When I'm receiving feedback:

- ➡ I'm not good at receiving feedback.
- ➡ I'm not good at receiving compliments.
- ➡ My manager or leader doesn't care about my development, so what's the point?
- ➡ I'm open to all feedback except from x.

These things happen automatically at an unconscious level, so it can be useful to bring them into your conscious awareness. Given that, consider these questions:

- ➡ What does the term feedback mean to you?
- ➡ When you hear the word feedback, how do you typically respond?

➡ When it comes to feedback, what do you believe to be true for you?

➡ When it comes to feedback, what do you believe to be true for others?

➡ How do these beliefs show up for you?

By becoming clear on your beliefs around feedback, you can consciously consider and evaluate if they're supporting you or getting in your way. If these beliefs are working for you, it's generally a good idea to leave them alone. If they're less useful, you may want to consider working with a coach or mentor to explore the ways in which you might change them.

# You get what you focus on

No one ever said 'I love difficult conversations'. But it's likely that we've all said to ourselves at one time or another, as either provider or receiver of feedback, 'This is going to be difficult.'

The human brain is full of neurons, nerves and structures, each responsible for different functions. When you have an experience, your neurons fire, neural connections strengthen and new connections start to form. The more you experience something, the stronger the connections, memories and beliefs become, which then influences what your brain will attend to in future. There are billions of bits of information you could pay attention to, but don't have the capacity to take it all in. This is where your reticular activating system (RAS) comes into play. Your RAS, a collection of nerves at your brainstem, creates a filter for what you focus on and then sifts through available data and presents you with the important bits that validate your thinking. Have you ever thought about buying a red car and then wondered why you keep seeing red cars, or learned a new phrase at a company meeting and then hear it everywhere? That's your RAS.

You get what you focus on, and if you go into a conversation with the narrative running in your head that 'this is going to be a disaster or confrontational', it's likely that will be the case. If you tell yourself 'I'm not good at giving or receiving feedback', it's likely to be the case. If you focus on feeling anxious, you're likely to get more of it. You get the picture. All of this leads to everyone putting up their defences and often disappearing into their heads to plan their next move. As a result, you stop listening to the other person and start listening to the voices in your head. In doing so you can inadvertently break rapport with the people you're in conversation with.

Now I'm not saying glide into every conversation fooling yourself into thinking it'll be easy, but if you can get clear on your desired outcome, whatever you'd like to achieve, you're more likely to focus on that and take meaningful action towards it. Given that, consider these questions:

➡ What's your desired outcome for this conversation?

➡ How do you want to show up in this conversation? (Calm, clear, present...)

You get what you focus on, and by changing that focus to something more accurate or something you want rather than something you're trying to avoid, you can begin to change the course of your feedback experiences.

# The human in front of you

I mentioned earlier that human beings can have both elegant and less elegant moments as they navigate the day-to-day. In your less elegant flashes, you can sometimes forget the other human being in front of you. You can find yourself under undue pressure to choose the right approach, to say the 'right' thing, act the 'right' way and thereby become preoccupied with not causing upset or doing something embarrassing. In all of this you forget one very simple but powerful step that can alleviate many of these feedback worries: you forget to ask the other person what works for them.

## Case study

I once sat with Sebastian, a leader I coach, who was concerned about giving his team some feedback as one project they were working on finished and another began. Seb went back and forth about what to say and how to make it fair. He wanted to keep them motivated. He was uneasy about how the team would react and didn't want them to be offended and walk away from the next project. He said he felt stuck and started to think about the ways in which he'd like someone to give him this feedback.

I asked him if he'd considered asking his team what they needed. 'It's about them, not you. The feedback is for them, and you want them to reflect on what you have to offer, so perhaps you could ask them what works for them?'

He paused and then repeated, 'It's not about me, it's about them. I'm going to ask them.' The next time I saw him, he had asked them and was pleasantly surprised by the conversations that followed and the change he felt as he realised he didn't have to have all the answers.

In doing this, you miss the opportunity to check what you or someone else might need in order to show up in the way they want to or participate in the feedback conversation. All of my research participants had preferences about the ideal way in which feedback could be delivered to them but none of them had shared this with anyone they get feedback from.

Many of them described 'just having to go with it'. But what if they didn't? If exchanging feedback provokes anxiety for all involved and you know your own unique magic formula to getting its delivery right, finding a way to share it can not only help recipients of feedback get what they need, it can also save providers of feedback from guessing and likely getting it wrong. Given that, consider these questions:

- ➡ How do you best receive feedback? For example, do you want to receive the feedback and discuss it immediately? Receive it in advance and have time to digest it before discussing it? Receive it and never discuss it?

- ➡ How do you want the feedback to be delivered? In writing, in person, both, on a call?

→ When feedback is shared, is there anything you'd find particularly useful or less useful?

When it comes to providing feedback, discovering the preferences of the recipient can save you time, effort and angst before, during and after. You can use the questions above to explore what might be useful for the person you're interacting with when it comes to receiving feedback. You can also answer the last question in relation to yourself – after all, you're also a human being with preferences who's engaged in the conversation.

When it comes to receiving feedback, advocating for what you need will help you get perspectives that you can interact with and not run away from. I can't promise that people will get it right every time, but I can promise that if you share what your preferences are for how you best receive feedback, they'll get it right for you more times than not.

# Putting it all together

Feedback is a two-way street, a conversation that begins with two humans saying hello to one another. To start to get an understanding of your relationship with feedback, you can answer any of the questions in this chapter. By sharing your learning with others, you can help them become clear on what you need and what works for you when it comes to exchanging feedback. It creates a sort of feedback contract or blueprint between you, designed around your needs and not a predefined process or approach. Imagine how differently your feedback conversations would go if two people could walk into a room and start by saying 'I'm feeling a little nervous about this and what would help me is...'

You don't need to wait for the next piece of feedback to be ready; you can start this conversation today. I've worked with people who have asked themselves these questions and then found an opportunity to share their preferences with their managers, leaders and colleagues in development conversations and over a coffee. It's also important to listen to their reply, taking a moment to recognise that what works for you may not be true for the person in front of you. In doing this, you can start to overcome some of the blockers that may have got in your way until now and realise that you're just two humans having a conversation. And the good news is we all know how to do that.

# Summary

- Feedback is a dialogue, not a monologue.

- The beliefs you hold about feedback influence how you interact with it – both how you receive and provide it.

- You get what you focus on; becoming clear on your desired outcome can help you take action towards it.

- If you can exchange feedback in a way that aligns with your preferences, you're more likely to interact with it productively and with purpose.

# 7

# Get curious, not furious!
# How to manage your state

Have you ever been on the receiving end of an email or message where you open it up, read the content and something you've read pushes your buttons? Before you know it, smoke is coming off your keyboard as you furiously type your reply and hit send – have that! The feeling of 'have that' is quickly erased by the feeling of palm hitting forehead and a heavy sigh as you think 'I probably shouldn't have done that.' It's normal and we all do it.

For us to make sense of each other's behaviour, we have to take it in and process it by unconsciously filtering what we're seeing or hearing based on our own values, beliefs and past experiences. This filtering process rapidly affects our thinking, our feelings and our physiology. What pops out the other side is our behaviour, and this whole process takes less than a millisecond. This explains why people can react very quickly to things and moments later, when their systems have calmed down, they have a slightly different response.

In emergency situations where immediate action is needed and appropriate, the speed of this processing and reaction can be incredibly helpful. In other moments, for the good of your wellbeing, relationships and career, you might want to get curious about what's going on for you and others and choose to respond rather than react. This all depends on your state.

Your state is your internal emotional condition; in effect, your state is like the emotional glue that holds a memory in place. The less emotional charge something you engage in has, the less likely it is that you'll be able to recall all the details of it, and vice versa. For example, can you remember taking the bins out two weeks ago? Unless you find this activity particularly exhilarating, the chances are you might only have a vague recollection of doing it. Whereas if you've had a less positive experience with feedback in the past, it's likely you'll be able to recall that with little or no prompting. In my research, I only needed to ask people 'What does feedback mean to you?' to see a range of effects.

It's important to know all of this when interacting with other people, as the reaction you have to something or get from others isn't always entirely down to the current situation. If this feedback conversation looks something like one you've had before that didn't go well, you can be catapulted back to that previous state. And when it comes to human emotions, more often than not, the strongest state wins.

As much as you might sometimes want to, you

can't control another person or their behaviours, but you can control and influence yours, and with practice that includes your state. In my research, participants described a range of emotions, thoughts and physical symptoms that they experienced before, during and after exchanging feedback.

## Research quotes

'I don't really know how to understand these feelings. So, I may feel the feelings of fear, the feelings of self-doubt, the emotions, the panic, and I panic with all these feelings – like I don't really know what to do with them.'

'Your body's screaming at you. And you say, "Oh, I'm dying. Oh, I have a heart problem" No, you don't; you have a bit of anxiety.'

'I get severe headaches and find it hard to focus on the conversation. If it's especially bad, I have to go home afterwards.'

'Normally I would either go bright red on my neck and cheeks or my leg would fidget. I tried wearing polo tops to cover my neck but then I just worry about getting a sweaty forehead.'

'I just withdraw into myself. It's like having two conversations in parallel. One with the person in front of me and one with myself in my head.'

'First I notice like a ball of energy in my chest and my breathing gets a bit faster. If I can stop it there that's great, but if not it's like that energy goes down my arms and into my hands. My hands start to ache and then I know I need to get up and walk away.'

For some people, these were more intense and stayed with them for days, while for others, they may have lasted a few minutes.

Becoming overwhelmed by our state when exchanging feedback can be tough for both the person providing it and the person receiving it. I once sat with a coachee who said she was so preoccupied with trying to stop her leg shaking that before she knew it, she'd agreed with all the feedback given to her and committed to 'corrective' actions. On reflection after the review, she felt quite differently but didn't feel she could do anything about it as the moment had passed.

When these states show up, there's a variety of different options available to help you to navigate them effectively. The participants in the research focused on using grounding techniques, but you can also consider the timing of feedback and consciously choosing the environment you're in when the feedback is given. These tools and options won't necessarily stop you having a reaction but they can help you and others to avoid becoming overwhelmed by it.

# Practical tools for managing your state

## Grounding techniques

When you have an unhelpful thought about something, your amygdala, the part of your brain responsible for emotional responses, kicks into action to tackle what's wrong. Something in your physiology changes and you notice, for example, that you start breathing faster or twitching your leg. This sends a signal back to your brain that gets interpreted as confirmation that there's something wrong, and the whole loop starts again.

Grounding techniques can help you to stay in the here and now. By focusing on your physicality or something in your surroundings, you can interrupt the looping thoughts and stop the cycle repeating. The great thing about many of these techniques is that you can try them without people noticing. You don't have to wait until your state is heightened to benefit from them and you can do them almost anywhere.

## Breathing

This has the single quickest impact on our physiology and behaviour and it's a great place to start when it comes to state management. There are a whole variety of breathing techniques available. Here are three of my favourites.

## Square breathing

1.  Start by sitting comfortably, with your feet on the floor.

2.  Breathe in through your nose, counting to four slowly in your head.

3.  Hold your breath for four seconds.

4.  Breathe out through your mouth, counting to four slowly in your head.

5.  Hold your breath for four seconds.

6.  Repeat steps two to five until you feel re-grounded.

**Watch out:** for some people, holding their breath and/or having to count during this technique can be distracting. If this is the case for you, you may prefer one of the following alternatives.

## Hand tracing

In this technique, to help regulate your breathing you're going to use the motion of tracing your hand as if you're drawing round it with a pen on a piece of paper.

1.  Start by sitting comfortably, with your feet on the floor, and take a few deep breaths.

2.  Hold your left or right hand out in front of you, palm facing down and fingers separated.

3.  Point out the index finger on your opposite hand. This is going to be your 'pen'. Put the tip of your finger at the base of your thumb where it meets your wrist.

4. As you begin to trace your hand up the outside of your thumb, breathe in.

5. As you trace back down the other side of your thumb, breathe out.

6. Continue this motion as you trace your hand, breathing in as you trace up and out as you trace down.

7. Concentrate on aligning the tracing motion with your breathing and find a rhythm that feels comfortable for you.

8. Repeat this rhythm as you trace across your hand at least three times.

With a small amount of practice, you can do this technique with the hand you're tracing gently resting on your knee, in your lap or on your desk.

You can also do this technique and replace the tracing of your hand with the imagery of a wave rolling in and out:

1. Start by sitting comfortably, with your feet on the floor, and take a few deep breaths.

2. Close your eyes and imagine you're sitting on your favourite beach watching the waves come in and go out.

3. As the next wave comes in, breathe in, and as it goes out, breathe out.

4. Don't hold your breath, just mirror the motion of the waves coming in and out, in and out, in and out.

5. Continue this rhythm for as long as you need: two minutes is usually a good amount of time to ground yourself.

6. When you're ready, open your eyes.

## Engaging your senses

Rather than becoming overwhelmed by worrying thought patterns, you can distract your mind in a variety of ways to focus on something outside of yourself. Engaging your senses can help to interrupt your thought spirals and ground yourself in the present moment.

### 5-4-3-2-1 technique

1. Wherever you're standing or sitting, start by taking a couple of deep breaths.

2. Look around you in the room you're in or outside the window and list, either out loud or in your head:

    ➡ five things you can see around you

    ➡ four things you can feel or touch (your chair, texture of your jumper, a table)

    ➡ three things you can hear around you (clock, traffic noise, birds)

    ➡ two things you can smell

    ➡ one thing you can taste.

3. Finish by taking another couple of deep breaths.

## Shape or colour sorting

Simply pick a colour or shape and notice how many things you can see around the room you're in or outside the window that match it. If you get to the end, and you're not suitably distracted, simply pick another colour or shape and have another go.

## Doodling

I once had a client who found that, when he felt overwhelmed by his thoughts and emotions, doodling was a great distraction. He took a small notebook and pen to his meetings and left one at his desk. If he needed a few minutes of distraction to ground himself, he'd draw small squares in the top right corner of the page. Of course, if you want to give this a go, the shape and location on the page is your choice!

# Movement

## Getting up and moving

If you notice yourself stuck in an unhelpful thought spiral, getting up, moving around and doing something else for a few minutes can stop the spiral. Getting up and moving can also help to process the flood of chemicals that gets released into our system when our fight, flight or freeze response is triggered. This movement could be as simple getting a drink, walking a lap of your office floor or going to the bathroom.

## Clenching your fists

By clenching and releasing your fists, you'll activate your muscles and your focus is drawn to the tension and relaxation that's created. You can also do this technique by scrunching up your toes and then stretching them out.

1.  If you're standing, rest your arms down by your sides. If you're sitting, you can rest your hands in your lap. Take a couple of deep breaths.
2.  Clench your fists into a tight ball and release, stretching out your hands and fingers as you do.
3.  Simply repeat this motion ten times.
4.  Finish by shaking out your hands, along with a couple of deep breaths.

One of the keys to using grounding techniques is finding the ones that are right for you by choosing one or two to experiment with and noticing the benefits. The bonus of these is that they can work in all situations where feeling grounded would be valuable, not just when exchanging feedback!

## Timing is everything

**Research quote**

'Timing is everything. Asking "Would you like some feedback on what I observed in our meeting just now?" gives the person getting the feedback a chance to prepare. Or request a rain check if they don't feel up to it.'

As you move through your day, switching contexts or tasks, jumping on the next call, going into the next meeting, you can do so without leaving the energy of the previous thing you did behind. You ask the polite 'How are you?' and get back the obligatory 'Good, thanks' and suddenly you're off – usually before you've had a chance to check in to see if you're in the best state you could be in to do the thing you're about to do.

If you don't pay attention to your state and stop to take an actual or metaphorical breath, you can end up pushing through your own warning signs and carrying on regardless. This usually leads to people having disproportionate reactions to what's going on in front of them, based on everything that may have built up inside them as they move through their day.

It doesn't have to be this way. I work with someone who schedules their meetings to start at five past the hour or half hour. The five minutes they give themselves are invaluable, giving them space to check in on basic human needs and take a few deep breaths to land in the next meeting. To help you be in the best state possible, it's useful to think about what happens immediately before and after you go into a feedback conversation. There's no right or wrong here, but there are some key things you can think about.

Given that, consider these questions:

→ What do you have planned for the five to ten minutes immediately before and after the conversation?

Many grounding techniques can be effective in only a few minutes and deliberately creating space for them can help you prepare beforehand and process afterwards. This can limit the amount of 'stuff' you carry into and out of the conversation.

➡ What time of day is the feedback conversation planned for?

Our energy, state and focus change throughout the day. It might be useful to have the conversation at the start of the day, the middle or the end of the day. This is something that can be mutually agreed between provider and recipient.

➡ When and how are you going to ask for feedback?

If you're going to request feedback, thinking about when and how you ask is crucial. Give the potential provider time to respond to the request, not react to it. If you ask someone to give you feedback on the spot, what you might get back is a not-so-tasty sandwich.

➡ What length of conversation is suitable?

I've worked in many organisations where a conversation that would benefit from an hour is optimistically scheduled for 30 minutes, and where what could be done in an email gets scheduled for 60 minutes. Consider what amount of time is most useful for the conversation you want to have, and make that time available. You may decide to split the conversation into two chunks – the first where the feedback is provided and any immediate questions are answered, followed by a second conversation to discuss the feedback further. This can be particularly helpful if either person likes to have time to reflect before responding.

Consciously thinking about the timing of feedback can help everyone prepare for the conversation and limit the surprise reactions that can happen if feedback requests or feedback conversations are sprung on someone. Remember that just because a conversation has been booked in the schedule doesn't mean it has to go ahead regardless. The key is to use the time, not fill the time. Sometimes the best thing you can do is delay or finish early, especially if someone's reaction isn't appropriate.

**Watch out:** there's a fine line here between delaying until you or others are in a better state and delaying to avoid the conversation.

To get through your immediate reaction to the feedback exchange or request, you need to give yourself permission to take time to sit with what you've heard. However, if you're metaphorically stuffing the feedback or feedback request into the bottom drawer of your desk and pretending it never happened, this might be easier said than done. The problem with leaving it too long is that people start to make up (probably inaccurate) stories and unhelpfully filling in all the gaps. You need to give yourself and others enough time to process, digest and make sense of what you've heard or said so you can start to choose how you want to respond and if you want to turn that feedback into some actionable steps.

## Location, location, location

### Research quote

'I once gave someone in my team feedback in a huge meeting room with a big table right down the middle. I didn't plan to be early, but I was by about five minutes, so I went and sat down opposite the door. When they came in, they looked a bit awkward and they made a joke about being on The Apprentice. They asked me if they were about to get the "you're fired" speech. We both laughed it off but that thought stayed with me for the rest of the day. Since then, we've agreed to do our performance chats in a coffee shop by the office – the whole thing just feels instantly more relaxed.'

Like timing, the environment you're in can also influence your state and behaviour in a helpful or less helpful way. The wrong environment can provoke feelings of stress and restlessness and become overwhelming or distracting. The right environment can support people to feel relaxed and open and maintain focus.

When it comes to exchanging feedback, environments that suggest formality or hint at organisational hierarchy are less ideal – the boss's office or conventional meeting rooms are a prime example. To avoid this, I've known people go to the other end of the scale and do the 'feedback drive-by', when they pop by someone's desk and do a 'surprise' download of the feedback to an unsuspecting recipient, sometimes in the presence of an audience.

In case you're reading this and thinking the only option left is sharing feedback in the stationery cupboard – hold on a minute. The good news is that if you've considered your answers to the questions in Chapter 6 and shared those with people you're exchanging feedback with, you've already done half the work.

Essentially, when it comes to feedback, the best environment is one where you can literally or meta-phorically sit or stand alongside someone and look at the thing together. Some of the most beneficial settings shared by participants in my research included sharing feedback over coffee or lunch, in meeting rooms with sofas and armchairs rather than tables and desks, standing at a whiteboard together, and outside during walking meetings. By using the relationship between state and environment you have an opportunity to choose the best environment to help you do the things you want to do.

# Putting it all together

There's no one universal formula for sharing feedback; every person will want or need something different. The minute you walk into a conversation thinking you know exactly how the other person will react is the minute they'll be a wonderfully creative human and do something totally out of left field.

A perspective only has an impact on you if you allow it to. In these moments you can't control the other person's reaction or responses, but you can choose and influence yours. When you enter a feedback exchange in the best possible state, you're more likely to have a productive conversation and get curious rather than furious.

By practising grounding techniques and finding the one or two that work for you, you'll notice how easily they fit into the rhythm of your day, allowing you to stay present when it matters. Consciously considering the timing and environment in which you share or request feedback will play a big part in its outcome for everyone involved.

## Summary

- ➡ You spend a lot of time preparing the content of feedback or *for* the content of the feedback – but how do you prepare yourself?

- ➡ Ask yourself whether the reaction you're having is from the current situation or whether you're being taken back to a previous experience with feedback that went badly. How do you want to respond now?

- ➡ Grounding techniques can help you to manage your state before, during and after the exchange. Which ones will you practise?

- ➡ The environment you're in and the timing of feedback can have a meaningful impact on your state. Small changes can make a big difference in your ability to be present and engage.

# 8

# Thoughts are not facts! Challenging your assumptions

It's really easy for humans to create stories; if you find a sliver of space in terms of meaning, you're likely to start filling in the gaps. Depending on the circumstances, these stories you tell yourself can be influenced by your history, past data and your own perception of right and wrong. Before you've even let a word escape your mouth, the chances are the storyline has started in your head. Every cell in your body hears everything you say, even when you don't say it out loud, and like your favourite children's book, the more you hear the story, the more it sticks.

Over time, you can become more and more convinced that the tales you tell yourself are non-fiction, and you saw in Chapter 6 the role that the RAS plays in this. You also become a supporting character in the stories of others, and if they're shared with you, they too can have an impact on your thinking. As a child, you might have been the shy kid; as a teenager, you might have been the difficult one; in your first job, you might have been the one with too much or too little ambition. People tell themselves all sorts of stories and make meaning of their own behaviour, skills and capabilities, their identity, the behaviour of others, what they would do if x happened, and more.

All the meaning-making and processing happens within someone's head; it's not immediately visible to those around them. So, when you interact with someone's behaviour, it becomes easy to infuse your own perception and assume the other person's intent before you've even said a word to them. You assume why they've done or not done something, why they reacted in a certain way, why they said what they said or what they might do next.

## Research quote

'I'm worried what she's going to voice. What's this topic going to be about? A lot of, you know, a lot of thoughts or ideas. Maybe it's because of what I did that day or it's the result of not doing something? I feel like this sucks all the air out of me and I'm just left with my own stories. I just feel like maybe I won't be able to work here anymore. Or I'm going to lose my job, or someone's going to replace me.'

As a result of the filtering process that you go through to take in the world around you, when you react, you respond to what you think has been said or done, not what was actually said or done. You're responding based on your interpretation of events and the whole thing is therefore subjective, not objective. This can cause a few challenges when it comes to feedback. The first is that, although the feedback is likely based on subjective data, it can come packaged as the truth with a dose of 'I'm just being honest'.

What you're really interacting with when feedback is shared is the perception or perspective of another person, and just because someone has a perspective, it doesn't make that perspective true, although it might be useful to consider. You only need to put the term 'optical illusions' into a search engine and share the results with friends to be reminded that a group of people can look at the same thing and reach very different conclusions. Have you ever spent time debating whether what you're looking at is a duck or a rabbit, a Grecian vase or a pair of faces looking at each other? None of these perspectives are wrong; they're just different, but you can invest your time and energy in trying to convince the other person that what you're seeing is right, and you do the same with feedback.

Rather than getting lost in assumptions or the back and forth of right vs wrong, which can lead people to becoming defensive, instead consider if the perspective is useful or not useful. The key to doing this is to create space to step into the shoes of the other person, to ask clarifying questions, to get real about your assumptions and to harness the power of 'What if...?'

# Stepping into someone else's shoes

Those debates about ducks or rabbits, Grecian vases or faces take on a different meaning when you take a step back, get curious and ask how they're seeing what they're seeing. Putting yourself in someone else's position can be incredibly helpful for providers of feedback, particularly when they're preparing what they want to share. It's equally valuable for people on the receiving end of feedback after the exchange has happened, to help them think through what they want to do next.

Of course, putting yourself in someone else's position doesn't mean you should overlook your own. Taking the time to really think about what's going on for you can help build greater self-awareness. That's why it's useful to put on your own shoes first, then the other person's, and then borrow a pair from a bystander who's not directly involved. However, standing in someone else's shoes can be easier said than done, so here are some effective questions you can ask yourself to get going.

Standing in your shoes:

➡ What am I experiencing? What did I see or hear?

➡ How do I feel about that?

➡ How does this impact me?

➡ How did I react? What did I say to myself?

➡ When x happens, what do I make it mean?

➡ What else could this mean?

- What do I need?

Stepping into the other person's shoes:

- How do you think they experienced or might experience this?
- How do you think they feel about this? Why would that be?
- How did they or might they react to it?
- What could have caused them to react or behave in this way?
- What else could this behaviour mean?
- How might they make meaning of this?
- What does the other person need?

Stepping into the shoes of a bystander:

- Looking from the outside in, what's going on here?
- What kinds of differences or similarities do you notice?
- How would someone not involved perceive this?
- What do you think either person needs?
- What advice would you give yourself?
- What would be a logical way forward?
- What are the three choices available to you next?

As the recipient, you might unknowingly dismiss how much effort the other person or people have put into preparing their feedback. You might not consider

how many performance reviews that person has had to write or deliver before they get to yours. As the provider, you might underestimate the impact and the weight that your perspective holds for the person on the receiving end.

You don't always need to ask yourself all these questions, but one or two at the right moment can help you to take a minute to build greater understanding and appreciation of the part you play in exchanging feedback.

# Asking questions for clarity

This can provide an opportunity to pause before jumping to conclusions and help us better understand where someone else is coming from. For some people, especially those who are experiencing feelings of anxiety, having space to ask questions is an important part of how they track and make sense of what they're hearing.

## Research quote

'I sometimes have trouble processing. So, I need it [feedback] to be as direct as possible. And I need to be able to ask clarification questions so that I can make sense of what you're saying before I leave and do anything else.'

When seeking clarity, it can be tempting to reach first for 'why' questions: why did you do that? Why did you say that? Why do you think that? Why questions can be incredibly confronting for some people, as they speak straight to our values. Essentially, these questions are asking why that thing is important to you, which, when it comes to feedback, can understandably lead to justification and defensiveness.

This justification goes both ways. People providing feedback can add in more and more content to validate the points they made in the first place, but this can lead to the original message becoming diluted. People receiving the feedback want to defend or explain their behaviour and, together, all this noise just preserves the ambiguity.

If anything about what you're exchanging is unclear, having the opportunity to ask clarifying questions can help you get more details so that you can choose what to do next. Here are some examples of questions you can ask to get clarity.

- Could you help me understand x?
- Can you tell me more about what you've observed?
- What was going on for you?
- When you said x, what I heard was y – is that correct?
- Can you give me another example? Can you give me some more examples?
- When did you first notice x?
- Can you elaborate on that?
- What did you mean when you said x?
- Tell me more about...
- Are there specific...?

➡ How specifically...? When specifically...? What specifically...?

➡ Can you explain x in another way?

These types of questions need to be asked with respect and curiosity and accompanied by a willingness from both provider and recipient to be open to the possibility that there's something one has seen that the other might not have noticed.

# Getting real about your assumptions

Mind reading means claiming to know the thoughts or feelings of someone else without specifying how you came to know the information. We all do it, and before we know it, these mind reads have worked their way into our interactions and the stories we tell ourselves. Someone looks in a certain direction when they're talking to us and we think they must be lying. Someone yawns during a presentation, so they must be bored. Someone sits with their arms folded in a meeting, so they must be grumpy. Now, all these things might be true, but they could also mean that someone's less keen on eye contact, someone's tired, that someone's cold – and a whole lot more.

During feedback conversations, you can make unhelpful meaning of what you're observing and attach that either to yourself or the other person. You've already seen one of the best examples of this in the third feedback myth (asking questions shows defensiveness). During my time working with various different people, some of the other common mind reads related to feedback conversations that have come up include the following:

➡ They didn't say anything; they don't care...

➡ They didn't make eye contact with me; they're not interested in what I have to say...

➡ I know I didn't come across well...

➡ I know they don't like me right now...

➡ I know they didn't really believe what they were saying...

➡ I know they were... frustrated, disappointed, angry...

It can be valuable to pay attention to the verbal and non-verbal cues that someone is giving you during a conversation, but it may not always be appropriate to stop every two seconds and say 'Hey, you crossed your arms, what's going on?' What you can do instead is pay attention to what goes on for you and what goes on for someone else without making meaning from it. This takes practice and a good place to start is to find a suitable people-watching spot, out of earshot of the content, and see what you notice when people are interacting.

Building up your ability to observe without making meaning can help you to pause before you create any unhelpful assumptions about yourself or others – and may just turn the novel you're writing in your own head into a more useful short story.

# The power of 'What if...?'

I've worked with many people who suffer from anxiety and one of the most common phrases they use is 'What if...?' 'What if I do something embarrassing? What if they say...? What if I don't... or what if I do...?' It's a phrase that also came up in the interviews I conducted in my first piece of research in relation to feedback. A few participants described it as a way to attempt to manage their feelings of anxiety by 'disaster planning' to mitigate against unhelpful things they thought might happen in the future. It's not something that's always said out loud; for some people it features heavily in their self-talk as they ruminate about upcoming events.

'What if...?' engages your imagination and when conducted in the negative can quickly become overwhelming. It can snowball and suddenly you're in Chapter 20 of an unhelpful story that's affecting your state and adding to feelings of anxiety rather than elevating them. When conducted in the positive, you can leverage the power of 'What if...?' in a constructive way to interrupt any unhelpful snowballing and come up with more choices and possibilities for yourself.

Here's how:

1. Start by writing down all your 'what ifs' in relation to feedback.

2. Review the list, one 'what if' at a time, and answer these questions:

    ➡ How likely or realistic is it that this thing will happen?

    ➡ What skills, resources or support do I have access to that can help me if it does?

# Putting it all together

Getting out of your head and therefore out of your own way when you're trying to do something is easier said than done. If you've chosen to give some of your time and energy to exchanging feedback, start by understanding where you and others are coming from. Doing this will allow you to meet someone where they are and not judge them from where you're standing, minimising any unhelpful meaning-making that might be going on.

Someone sharing their perspective is just another person saying to you 'Here's how I saw it'. And, of course, logically, we all know that nobody sees the world as we do; that's the wonderful uniqueness of humans. On a logical level you accept that you see something differently from me, but on an emotional level it's different. So if you do notice yourself making unhelpful meanings or assumptions, take the time to be curious and ask a question to clarify what you're seeing, hearing or feeling and avoid adding an extra novel to the library in your head.

# Summary

- ➡ Other people might respond to what they think you've said or done, not what you've actually said or done.

- ➡ Just because someone has a perspective doesn't mean it's true or accurate, but it may be useful to consider for the benefit of your own learning, development and performance.

- ➡ Asking questions for clarity and standing in the shoes of others can help you build greater self-awareness, gain better understanding of their point of view and get the clarity you need to move forward.

- ➡ Everyone can make unhelpful assumptions about themselves and others. Before responding or reacting, take a moment to consider your answer to the question, how do you know what you know?

# 9

# Don't 'should' all over yourself! Rediscovering your choices

I should know what to do. I should know the answer. I should know better. I should just do it. I should have done it differently. I shouldn't care so much. I shouldn't get anxious. I should just brush it off. I shouldn't get so emotional. I shouldn't need to tell them. I should just get on with it. I shouldn't need reassurance. I should just tell them. I shouldn't worry...

If you recognise any of these statements as words you have said or words that have been said to you, before doing anything else ask yourself 'Should according to whom?' The word 'should' creates psychological pressure to act. When you use 'should' statements or let others do the same, you can obscure the fact that you have a choice. If you succumb to this pressure, you can end up throwing your efforts into taking a bunch of actions, but not necessarily meaningful actions that take you towards your desired outcomes.

Going back to the origin of the word feedback in the context of electrical engineering, one of the early definitions (by American computer scientist Norbert Wiener) is: 'Feedback is a method of controlling a system by reinserting into it the result of its past performance.' Despite all the new models and fancy extra words we can put around the different types of feedback, in practice we haven't moved on much from this old definition. We're still trying to control something: behaviour, reactions and actions. In my view, the provider of feedback is often trying to control the reactions of the other person or use feedback as a way to shape other people into what they believe they should be. The recipient is trying to control themselves, and any feedback processes in place are trying to control everyone involved.

## Research quote

'Feedback will often come from colleagues via surveys. It's collated and you're compared to every other person, then told all the things you should be doing. It's dreadful and truly unhelpful. People can make comments they wouldn't say to your face if it's anonymous. You've no idea about the context of the comment. It will be covering a period of time and about nothing you might be able to control or change even if you want to.'

Feedback isn't about 'should' or 'control'; it's about choice. It's about inspiring a different perspective on something and creating choice for the person receiving it. That starts with everyone knowing their desired outcome, for providers to really know what they're giving and for recipients to understanding what they're getting.

# Know your desired outcome

A brilliant question once offered to me by one of my mentors was 'If you don't know why you're doing it, why are you doing it?' Our time is a precious resource and we all know this, but that doesn't stop us busying ourselves with any and all activities and actions for fear of missing out. By knowing your desired outcome when seeking and sharing feedback, you become aware of the difference between where you are and where you want to get to. This can allow you to focus your efforts and energy with purpose. Given that, consider these questions:

As the provider:

- ➡ What's the outcome you want from sharing feedback?
- ➡ What do you want to achieve?
- ➡ For what purpose do you want to achieve this?
- ➡ How will you know you've achieved this?
- ➡ What do you not want to achieve?
- ➡ What support or resources do you need to get your outcome?

**Watch out:** if your answer to either of the first questions is anything like 'To tell the other person what I think of them because I can't contain it anymore' or 'Because I have frustrations to get off my chest', now might not be the right time.

As the receiver:

➡ What's the outcome you want from seeking feedback?

➡ What specifically do you want feedback on?

➡ When do you want it? Why?

➡ Who do you want to seek feedback from? Yourself, manager, colleague?

➡ What will happen if you get it? What won't happen if you get it?

➡ What support or resources do you need to get your outcome?

**Watch out:** if your answer to the first question is anything like 'Because someone told me I have to', now might not be the right time.

It's important that our desired outcomes are just that – ours. Not the 'have to' and 'should' belonging to someone else. In my second study, 76 per cent of participants said they get feedback because it's a 'have to'. Before investing your energy and resources, make sure you know what you're investing them in.

# For providers: know what you're giving

At work with our colleagues, at home with our families or when out with our friends, I think everybody can relate to that moment of thinking 'Why haven't they just done the thing I asked them to do?' The real starting question here is 'How clear was I when I asked them to do it?'

If what you're offering someone comes without a genuine 'do what you like with it', the chances are it's not feedback. Instead, it's likely to be a direction or an instruction positioned as feedback, which comes with a consequence. It's understandable that these things get muddled as the people providing instructions or directions want to avoid causing a drama and coming across as micromanaging or too direct. So, instructions get dressed up as feedback and then the person who offers it gets grumpy when the receiver doesn't do that thing. Feedback isn't a call to action, so it's important to know what you're giving.

**Direction**: You're telling the person what action to take and clearly explaining the consequence of doing or not doing it. You may work with them to plan how they'll take the action. It's likely that there's a detrimental consequence to not doing it.

**Instruction**: You're outlining the specific steps you want someone to take. There might be a detrimental consequence to not following these steps.

**Perspectives**: You're sharing what you're seeing, hearing or feeling from your point of view. The person receiving your perspectives can choose what they do with them.

If you're unclear about this upfront, it's likely to cost you time and energy further down the road, and those people dramas you were looking to sidestep will come up anyway. For the good of your future self and out of respect for others, if the thing is a 'have to', let them know. If there's a consequence to doing or not doing the thing in the way described, let them know. If the thing will have a detrimental consequence on their professional outcomes – you guessed it, let them know.

# Language of necessity vs possibility

Once you're clear about what you're giving – direction, instruction or perspectives – it's time to get clear with your language. For providers of feedback, it's especially important to consider when your language suggests choice and when it doesn't, and how this relates to what you're giving the other person.

Language that implies necessity, such as should, shouldn't, must, mustn't, need, have to, is best used when providing directions or instructions. Language that implies possibility or choice, such as can, can't, could, couldn't, will, won't, possible, impossible is best used when providing a perspective.

If you know what you're giving, you can clearly communicate it to the other person instead of implying choice where there is none and 'have to' where there's choice.

# For recipients: know what you're getting

There's a shared responsibility between you and the person offering you something to establish what it is you're getting. In one sense, if you've approached people to ask for their perspectives rather than wait for them to come to you, this is easy. To help you know what you're getting, the first step is to use the clarifying questions from Chapter 8.

If you've asked for people's perspectives, and that's what you get, the second step is to thank them. As you know by now, providing perspectives can be equally as anxiety inducing for the people giving them. No matter what people say, don't argue. You sought their perspective and that's what you've received; it's up to you what you do with it next.

---

### Case study

I once worked with someone who said, 'There should be constructive feedback. They just told me I was doing an excellent job. There's no feedback. What am I supposed to do with that?' My reply was, 'Give yourself a high five.'

In truth, there might always be things we can improve or be better at. The key question is: for what purpose?

---

# The choice is yours

I've said it before and I'll say it again: feedback is not a call to action and there are a variety of things you could choose as your next step.

➡ If you don't agree with the perspectives, put them to one side (or in the bin).

➡ Look for the themes in the perspectives. Do these themes resonate with you and if so, what, if anything, would you like to do?

➡ Seek out a second, or better yet a third, opinion.

➡ You could do nothing.

➡ Decide if there are any changes you want to make and create some actionable steps.

➡ Consider how often you've heard this information before.

In my second research study, 87.5 per cent of respondents said that they reflect on the feedback they receive and act only on the points they think are relevant. Leveraging perspectives can be a powerful way to gain new learnings, insights and highlight any lack of awareness. What you do with them in support of your development and desired outcomes is your choice.

> **Research quote**
>
> 'The ability to build my own feedback requests and send them to targeted individuals means I can do it when I wish and ensure a spread of recipients that avoids bias, so I then have real insight into others' perspectives. Then I get to choose what I do with them.'

# Putting it all together

It's easy to fill your language with 'I should' and 'I must', but I'd suggest a more useful question to start with is: do you want to? If you're operating under the belief that you have to act, it creates psychological pressure and limits your choices. When you're providing feedback to someone else, you need to be sure that what you're giving is actually feedback, in order to give yourself and others the best possibility to get what you all want. When receiving feedback, you need to be clear about what your choices are so you can decide which steps, if any, you want to take next. For both provider and receiver, this starts with simply defining the desired outcome.

# Summary

- ➡ Don't 'should' all over yourself or others – it creates unnecessary psychological pressure and anxiety.

- ➡ Know your desired outcome so you can orientate your actions towards it.

- ➡ As a provider of perspectives, know what you're giving and provide clarity as you do so.

- ➡ As the receiver of perspectives, know what you're getting and what your choices are.

# 10

# Words can do funny things to people! The conscious use of language

The great thing about language is that it allows us to communicate with other people. The challenge with language is that we think we're communicating clearly with other people. Words are semantically packed, and they do funny things to people. They can provoke memories, emotions and reactions. They can inspire curiosity and engagement or cause us to retreat and become guarded. In general, this is true of any word or combination of words, but in my experience of working in organisations, some are more provocative than others: power, fairness, change, transparency and resilience, to name a few. The same is true of the word feedback; get any group of people together and simply say the word feedback and watch what happens to them.

I once sat with a client who found the word feedback particularly provoking. It was difficult for them to talk through what they wanted to say to their team because they kept getting hung up on the word itself. For the benefit of our conversation, I suggested that perhaps we could just replace the word feedback with the word cushion. This has no scientific foundation – it was simply the closest object to them at the time. Although I suspect they thought the suggestion was bonkers, it was amazing how taking one word out of the conversation gave this person space to breathe and think about what it was that they wanted to say.

When you're talking to someone, just because a word pops into your head doesn't mean it should come out of your mouth. Words matter and, while you can say you have good intent, you can still cause an unhelpful unintended impact. Now, if you continuously think too long and hard about the words you use, linguistic structures and language preferences, I'm not sure you'd ever talk to another human being again. Consciously using language when it really counts can be the difference that makes a difference to a productive and meaningful conversation.

For people who experience any anxiety around feedback, one of the biggest challenges they referenced in relation to language was ambiguity and vagueness. There are any number of avenues through which you can explore language, but when it comes to feedback and taking learnings from my research, the three key aspects to consider are: framing, common language traps and being clear when it counts.

# Framing

The frame you put around something can entirely change your own and other people's interpretation and experience of it. If you've ever been asked 'Do you have a minute?' and an hour later you're still there in discussion, you probably get what I mean. There are many opportunities where framing can be useful to help you think; for example, a frame can be as simple as the subject line of an email or the title on a meeting invite.

Often the framing is so clear to you that you forget to give it to other people. 'Surely it's obvious?' you might say to yourself, but the minute that anyone says 'Surely it's obvious?' is the minute they already have doubt in their own mind. And not giving a clear frame around something can lead to unintentional effects.

## Research story

'Late in the day, I had a Teams meeting invite from my line manager for the following day – 15 minutes, and all it said was 'quick catch-up'. And that got me, you know, all over the place. And I don't know why. I'd done nothing wrong, but it was like, what do they want to talk about? I thought, well, if it was anything to worry about, surely it wouldn't be just in a cryptic, quick catch-up type meeting? But, you know, I'm thinking, should I reply to this? Should I ask him? Should I prepare anything, but what?

'It was late and I was at home, so I didn't check. It wasn't pleasant; it played on my mind all evening. I just wanted to get it over and done with. And the funny thing is, it was to offer me a pay rise. It's interesting, isn't it, the things that we can do with a bit of ambiguity?'

The two most helpful frames you can use when sharing feedback are known as the outcome frame and the backtrack or clarity frame.

# The outcome frame

This is our opportunity to state as clearly as possible the answer to the question 'For what purpose?' In the example above, instead of the meeting invite being labelled as 'quick catch-up', it could easily become 'pay rise chat' or 'pay rise update'. When working out what the outcome frame would be for the thing you're doing, the answers to all or any of the following questions will help you determine what to communicate.

1. What's my desired outcome?
2. For what purpose are we having this conversation, meeting, email?
3. What do I want to happen or not happen during the conversation?

# The backtrack frame

This can be used to check and clarify information and meaning and is a great way to uncover any unintended mix-ups. Used during or at the end of feedback conversations, backtracking and summarising what you've heard can build rapport and help you both move on from the same point of reference. When using the backtrack frame, it's important to remember that what you see and hear is your interpretation of what the other person did. Here are some ways in which you can introduce backtracking while owning your own perspective.

1. What we've discussed is abc, and what we've agreed as next steps are xyz.

2. When you talked about x, what I heard was y. Did I understand that correctly?

3. When you talked about x, to me it meant y. Is that what you meant?

The outcome frame can help you in your preparation for feedback and during any feedback exchanges. Using the backtrack frame can help convey that you've been listening to the other person and to check your understanding before you take any next steps.

# Avoiding language traps

Whether you're providing feedback to someone or receiving it, talking out loud, or talking to yourself in your head, there are three common language traps you could fall into, and they involve the words 'try', 'but' and 'don't'.

## Try

This is an interesting word. If you looked it up in the dictionary, it would have a variety of definitions attached to it. Despite this, in day-to-day conversation, 'try' has become a nicety, a politeness that doesn't really mean much at all. It is often used to signal good intentions, but it's also used to signal false ones, which can lead to misunderstandings and disappointments. When you invite someone to a social event and the reply you get is 'I'll try to come', everyone knows that this likely means the person won't show up. In this instance, people use the word 'try' to buy themselves or others a bit of space and comfort by avoiding saying no directly. This can create confusion, especially in work contexts where people are asking for things from each other. When you hear 'I'll try and get that done by Friday', what does that actually mean? Will they, or won't they? The lack of directness in the reply can create uncertainty for the person making the request. Similarly, when you ask someone 'Could you try and work on this?' and the reply you get is 'Yes', what expectation does that create for what the other person is going to do?

Here are some examples of suggested alternatives you can use:

- ➡ I can't get that done by x. Would Monday be acceptable?
- ➡ I need this by x – is there anything you need from me to make that possible?
- ➡ Is there any support you need to practise/work on y?
- ➡ I will begin..., I will stop..., I will start...
- ➡ I do..., I don't...
- ➡ I can..., I cant...

In the immortal words of the wise green alien Yoda: 'Do or do not. There is no try.'

## But

The word 'but' is particularly problematic when you're exchanging feedback with someone. 'But' is like a giant language trap door that everything you say before it falls into, and what people are left with is anything you've said after it. Here are some examples. See how these land with you:

- ➡ I care about your development, but I don't have time to talk to you right now.

- ➡ I want to hear your ideas, but can you hold onto them until our next conversation?

- ➡ You did a great job in that meeting, but next time perhaps give others a chance to speak more.

- ➡ You make a good point, but I'm not going to consider your perspective.

- ➡ I get that this is frustrating for you, but can I make a suggestion?

Where you can, replace the word 'but' with 'and'. Using 'and' maintains rapport and avoids the trap door effect: 'I get that this is frustrating for you and can I make a suggestion?' It might not always be relevant to replace 'but' with 'and'. In these instances, you can consider using a full stop instead: 'I care about your development. I don't have time to talk to you right now.'

These subtle changes can help ensure that people have the best chance of hearing the message as you intend, even if they make their own meaning of it.

## Don't

Your brain has a really hard time hearing negations in language, so when you say 'don't', what you often hear is 'do'. If I said to you, 'Don't think of a blue elephant with pink spots', what your brain hears is 'Think of a blue elephant with pink spots'. How many times have you said out loud 'I don't mind...' but in your head you're saying 'I flipping do mind...'

When you're interacting with feedback, there are many don'ts that can come up and what you hear is likely to be the opposite.

| *What you say:* | *What you hear:* |
|---|---|
| Don't get anxious... | Get anxious... |
| Don't get defensive... | Get defensive... |
| Don't rush... | Rush... |
| Don't get upset... | Get upset... |
| Don't mess this up... | Mess this up... |
| Don't forget to say... | Forget to say... |

Instead of unintentionally focusing on what you don't want to have happen, say it the way you do want it to happen: 'I want to be calm', 'I want to remember to say', 'I want to be clear'. Your unconscious mind will take the path of least resistance and you're much more likely to get the thing you want if you simply say it the way you want it. Even the subtle change in your framing from 'feedback meeting' to 'feedback conversation' can be incredibly powerful for everyone involved. It takes away the potential formality of a meeting and frames it the way you want it to be – a conversation.

# Being clear when it counts

I often get asked to look through the feedback someone has been given and assist them to make sense of it. I've also supported people who are keen to develop in a particular way to work out how to get the perspectives of others to help them do this. In both cases, things get really interesting when people mix the language of possibility and necessity, as you saw in the previous chapter, and fall into all of the language traps I've just described.

## Feedback example

'I think it was OK overall, but x could be better. Have a think about possibly doing y next time. If you could try that, it would be great – it might make a difference.'

## Feedback request example

'Sorry to bother you. I'm looking to develop x and wondered if you could give me some feedback. It would mean a lot if you could try to get this back to me by the end of the week, but I know you're busy, so no worries if not.'

It's likely that you're reading these two examples and thinking 'What has either person truly said or asked for?' Feedback and feedback requests presented in this way are not uncommon, so it's understandable when people feel anxious, uncomfortable or unclear about what it is they're trying to say. A strategy used by one of my research participants is to write out the things they want to say and put them to one side for a couple of hours or overnight. Going back to it with a fresh perspective means that they're clear and confident in what they want to send.

# Putting it all together

Language is an incredible tool that people use to interact with the world around them. Although words come with their own definitions, in reality they can mean subtly different things to different people. Overthinking and over-crafting your communication isn't the answer, as this can come across as inauthentic, but you can be conscientious and use language consciously to help you communicate as clearly as possible when it counts. By using framing and avoiding some of the common language traps, you can help direct people's attention to your desired outcome and minimise any ambiguity that might cause anxiety or uncertainty.

# Summary

- ➥ Be clear when it counts.

- ➥ Framing can help you clarify your goal, give focus to your conversation and minimise ambiguity.

- ➥ Backtracking and summarising can support you in maintaining rapport, getting clarity and showing people you've been actively listening to them.

- ➥ You're much more likely to get the outcome you want if you focus on what you do want and say it the way you want it to be said.

# Part 4

## Your new relationship with feedback

# 11

# Putting it all into practice: perspectives and possibilities

What if you called feedback 'perspectives'? What if you said hello to the human in front of you and just had a conversation? What if you used perspectives to create possibilities?

Feedback might be hard; perspectives don't have to be. As inspired by reflections from Eleanor Roosevelt, 'No one can make you feel inferior without your consent.' The most significant thing you can do to change your relationship with feedback is to leave the word itself behind you. Instead, invest your time and energy in using perspectives to open possibilities. Perspectives aren't right or wrong, true or false; they just are. No two perspectives are the same, so what you have to offer and what you can gain from the way others see things is incredibly valuable. This applies to the pursuit of your goals as well as your career.

It's now up to you to take it from page to practice.

As you've progressed through this book, the chapters have looked at the good, the bad and the ugly of some common feedback models and seven feedback myths that often show up in organisations. You've learned that there's no one-size-fits-all when it comes to feedback. I then shared practical tools and strategies to support you in redesigning your relationship with perspectives.

It's just two humans having a conversation, and now you have a series of questions you can answer to discover your preferences and beliefs around exchanging feedback. Doing this will give you a great blueprint to share with others in your organisation to ensure you can share and receive perspectives in a way that's right for you. To get started, ask yourself the following question:

**What does the term feedback mean to me?**

I explored managing your state, including a selection of tools, tips and techniques to manage it, including breathing, noticing, distraction and movement techniques. I also explored the importance and influence of timing and environment when it comes to exchanging feedback. To get started, ask yourself:

**What do I need to do to help myself be in the best state possible to exchange perspectives?**

I challenged your assumptions, explored the stories that humans tell themselves and showed you how to step into someone else's shoes. I went on to look at asking questions for clarity and at leveraging the power of the question 'What if...?' To get started, ask yourself:

**What are the stories I tell myself about feedback?**

Rediscovering your choices was all about how to clarify your outcome for providing or receiving perspectives. As the provider, are you clear about what you're giving: direction, instruction or perspective? As the recipient, are you clear about what your choices are once you receive the perspectives? To get started, ask yourself:
**What's my desired outcome for seeking or sharing perspectives?**

I looked at the conscious use of language and highlighted the impact of being vague or ambiguous with language when sharing feedback. I showed you how to use framing to create clarity and how to avoid some of the most common language traps – but, try and don't – that you can inadvertently fall into. To get started, ask yourself:
**Where can I be stronger with my framing to create clarity for others?**

Whether you're the provider or receiver, or both, the key to this is practice. The more you can practise, the more you'll realise you can do this thing that you might have been hiding from until now. Focus on the first thing first and then incrementally build on each success as you go. As a starting point you could:

- → revisit the contents page to see which chapters have stayed with you or that jump out at you, as this will give you a good indication of where to start with any practical steps you want to take

- → answer the questions from Chapter 6 and share the answers with your manager or leader

→ pick one of the state management tools and practise it for one or two weeks to see what impact it has on your overall state.

So far, I've been talking about changing your relationship with perspectives at work. The tools, strategies and techniques I've shared with you can be adapted to almost any environment where you're working on an outcome, exchanging perspectives at home, in education settings, or at recreational clubs. I wonder where you'll take it...?

Feedback might be the thing you've built it up to be, or the thing you've been told it is – but not anymore. If you've had an unhelpful experience on either side of the feedback conversation, you might now understand why that happened and you can choose how you want to go forward from here.

And the next time that someone asks you 'Can I offer you something?', remember that you now have a variety of options for responding. You can help them understand your relationship with perspectives and coach them to provide it to you in a way that's most beneficial for you. You can ask someone how they feel about this thing before you offer it to them, and finally you can also remember that one appropriate answer to 'Can I offer you something?' is 'No'.

After you've read this book, I hope you'll be inspired to reimagine your relationship with feedback and make it more purposeful for you and others. Ask yourself again: What if you called feedback 'perspectives'? What if you said hello to the human in front of you? What if you used perspectives to create possibilities?

After all, it's just two humans having a conversation.

# References

Amy (2016) 'Blogging my way to recovery'. Mind, 18
August. URL: mind.org.uk/information-support/
your-stories/blogging-my-way-to-recovery

Andlin-Sobocki, P, Jönsson, B et al (2005) 'Cost of
disorders of the brain in Europe'. *European Journal
of Neurology*, 5 May. URL: doi.org/10.1111/j.1468-
1331.2005.01202.x

Belschak, F D & Hartog, D N D (2009) 'Consequences
of positive and negative feedback: The impact
on emotions and extra-role behaviors'. *Applied
Psychology*, 5 March. URL: doi.org/10.1111/j.1464-
0597.2008.00336.x

Bhattarai, M D (2007) 'ABCDEFG IS – the principle of
constructive feedback'. *Journal of Nepal Medical
Association*, 1 July. URL: doi.org/10.31729/jnma.293

Bock, W (2018) 'Wally Bock's three star leadership: The 4
R's of receiving feedback'. URL: threestarleadership.
com/personal-development/the-4-rs-of-receiving-
feedback

Bracken, D W, Rose, D S & Church, A H (2016)
'The evolution and devolution of 360°
feedback'. *Industrial and Organizational
Psychology*, 29 December. URL: doi.org/10.1017/
iop.2016.93

Broderick, V (2023) '5 Frameworks for giving
effective feedback and reducing your

stress'. URL: vaughanbroderick.com/
frameworks-for-giving-effective-
feedback

Brown, N (2021) 'The curious (and completely flawed)
case of the positivity ratio'. TalentQ, 21 September.
URL: talent-quarterly.com/the-curious-and-
completely-flawed-case-of-the-positivity-ratio

Champion Health (2024) 'The workplace health
report'. URL: championhealth.co.uk/wp-content/
uploads/workplace-health-report-2024.pdf

Ferguson, A C (2014) '"Positivity ratio" research
now subject to an expression of concern'.
Retraction Watch, 29 July. URL: retractionwatch.
com/2014/07/29/positivity-ratio-research-now-sub-
ject-to-an-
expression-of-concern

Fleenor, J W & Prince, J M (1997) 'Using 360-degree
feedback in organizations: an annotated bibliogra-
phy'. URL: eric.ed.gov/?id=ED413627

Fortune Business Insights (March 2024) '360 degree
feedback software market size & growth
[2030]'. URL: fortunebusinessinsights.com/360-de-
gree-feedback-software-market-104481

Friedman, H L & Brown, N J L (2018) 'Implications
of debunking the "critical positivity ratio" for
humanistic psychology: Introduction to special
issue'. *Journal of Humanistic Psychology*, 29 March.
URL: doi.org/10.1177/0022167818762227

HR News (2022) 'Workplace stress and anxiety leads to
productivity drop'. 25 January. URL: hrnews.co.uk/
workplace-stress-and-anxiety-leads-to-productivity-
drop

Joseph, R (ed.) (2021) 'What to do if you feel too anxious to work'. Priory, 10 February. URL: priorygroup.com/blog/what-to-do-if-you-feel-too-anxious-to-work

Kluger, A N & DeNisi, A S (1996) 'The effects of feedback interventions on performance: A historical review, a meta-analysis, and a preliminary feedback intervention theory'. *Psychological Bulletin*. URL: doi.org/10.1037/0033-2909.119.2.254

Losada, M & Heaphy, E (2004) 'The role of positivity and connectivity in the performance of business teams'. *American Behavioral Scientist*. URL: doi.org/10.1177/0002764203260208

Marcin, M & Nemeroff, C B (2003) 'The neurobiology of social anxiety disorder: The relevance of fear and anxiety'. *Acta Psychiatrica Scandinavica*, 29 August. URL: doi.org/10.1034/j.1600-0447.108.s417.4.x

NICE (2013) 'Social anxiety disorder: Recognition, assessment and treatment'. NICE, 22 May. URL: nice.org.uk/guidance/cg159/chapter/Introduction

Razzetti, G (2023) 'The five R's of feedback: A blueprint for personal and team growth'. *Fearless Culture – Reimagining Work*, 23 July. URL: gustavorazzetti.substack.com/p/the-five-rs-of-feedback-a-blueprint

Sherf, E (2023) 'How to deliver feedback that lasts'. URL: kenan-flagler.unc.edu/perspectives/the-3cs-how-to-deliver-feedback-that-lasts

Vincent, P V (2023) 'Social anxiety disorder'. Patient, 29 September. URL: patient.info/mental-health/anxiety/social-anxiety-disorder

Westwood, R (2023) 'Can I offer you something? Examining how people with social anxiety disorder experience feedback in the workplace'. Essex

University, 30 January. URL: doi.org/10.31234/osf.io/xazf9

Wittchen, H, Stein, M B & Kessler, R C (1999) 'Social fears and social phobia in a community sample of adolescents and young adults: Prevalence, risk factors and co-morbidity'. *Psychological Medicine*, 1 March. URL: doi.org/10.1017/s0033291798008174

World Health Organization (2023) 'Anxiety disorders'. 27 September. URL: who.int/news-room/fact-sheets/detail/anxiety-disorders

Zenger, J (2018) 'Your employees want the negative feedback you hate to give'. *Harvard Business Review*, 15 January. URL: hbr.org/2014/01/your-employees-want-the-negative-feedback-you-hate-to-give

## Useful resources

- ➡ Anxiety Care UK: anxietycare.org.uk
- ➡ Anxiety UK: anxietyuk.org.uk/anxiety-type/social-anxiety
- ➡ British Association for Counselling and Psychotherapy (BACP): bacp.co.uk
- ➡ Calm: calm.com
- ➡ Headspace: headspace.com
- ➡ Mind: mind.org.uk; infoline: 0300 123 3393
- ➡ Free resources to support staff mental health: mind.org.uk/workplace/mental-health-at-work/taking-care-of-your-staff/useful-resources

# Acknowledgements

Like feedback, writing a book is rarely a solo adventure.

I first want to thank Sue Richardson and the team at The Right Book Company for their expertise and guidance in the publishing of this book.

To my colleagues past and present, friends and family, thank you for being a constant source of reassurance, humour, encouragement and wise counsel.

I'm immensely grateful to the individuals who inspired my research and the participants who so generously contributed their time and personal experiences. It was a privilege to hear and learn from your stories.

Thank you.

# About the author

Becky is an organisational psychologist with more than 17 years' experience training and coaching in a variety of industries across the UK, US and Europe. She's a qualified trainer and coach and holds an MSc in psychology.

Her career in training and development started with in-house roles in the retail and aerospace sectors before she set up her own training and coaching consultancy in 2016. It was in this role that she began to specialise in working with individuals with anxiety, particularly social anxiety. In 2021, she joined Monkey Puzzle Training and Consultancy, where she now works as an organisational psychologist, coach, trainer and chief experience officer.

Becky's specialist research area is in social anxiety and how it manifests in the workplace, including how it impacts feedback, imposter syndrome, burnout and psychological safety.

Championing diversity and inclusivity has always been a core element of her work and she's involved with a number of UK charitable organisations, including Diversity Role Models, as an LGBTQ+ role model providing support to young LGBTQ+ people.